Generous Giving

LESSONS ON CHRISTIAN STEWARDSHIP

Dr. Jeffrey P. Pedersen

Copyright © 2020 by Dr. Jeffrey P. Pedersen

All rights reserved. No part of this publication may be reproduced, distributed or transmitted in any form or by any means, including photocopying, recording, or other electronic or mechanical methods, without the prior written permission of the publisher, except in the case of brief quotations embodied in critical reviews and certain other noncommercial uses permitted by copyright law. For permission requests, write to the publisher, addressed "Attention: Permissions Coordinator," at the address below.

Pedersen/New Harbor Press
1601 Mt. Rushmore Rd, Ste 3288
Rapid City, SD 57701
www.newharborpress.com

Generous Giving/Dr. Jeffrey P. Pedersen —1st ed.
ISBN 978-1-63357-368-0

Thank you to Maria Pedersen

Contents

INTRODUCTION 1

THE ONION 7

TWO TREES 17

SACRAMENTAL GOD 25

100% 33

THE HOLY SPIRIT & THE CHURCH 41

GENEROSITY 53

TIME 61

SOCIETY 69

WORK 77

INVESTMENTS 85

BIBLIOGRAPHY 97

INTRODUCTION

WHEN WE LIVE WHAT we believe, we have an innate passion to support the causes of Christ. Faith is a gift created by the Holy Spirit dwelling in us, the essence of living the Christian life. It is the Holy Spirit that inspires people to be the Church, and transforms the greed in our hearts to generosity. Our giving will never exceed our faith. When our actions stem from a carnal mind, rather than inspiration from the Holy Spirit, we give half-heartedly or out of reluctant obligation at best. We have no want for God, nor for living the Christian life. Still, God calls to share our lives.

As we grow in relationship with the Holy Spirit, we too grow in our generous giving. We experience the joy and inner satisfaction of giving our lives for the sake of Jesus and others. Jesus said that if anyone wanted to be His followers, they must pick up their crosses and follow Him. As Jesus was sacrificed on a cross, His pain and suffering brought us reconciliation and peace. For us to carry the cross means suffering and pain, but it also means victory and life. It's in this victory that we experience the joy of salvation. The joy we have in God is the joy that we share generously with others in many and various ways.

I know people who both have a lot and give a lot. I know others who have very little, but also share what little they have. No matter their means, generous people always make a difference in the lives of others. I know a man who lives in a modest house, but also owns the modest houses that are adjacent to him, and the one across the street from where he lives. He lets needful families live in these modest homes rent-free. He may not have much, but he is rich in mercy. The families he helps are more valuable to him than all the riches of the world.

Throughout my years as a pastor, I've been touched by the creative ways our church members have found in contributing to our mission and supporting our work. One man never failed to plow the snow from the church parking lot after a blizzard, others donated their expertise as plumbers, carpenters, or electricians to help families in need; while another woman used her extensive musical training to enrich our worship services. Others have embarked on mission trips to inner city neighborhoods, donating tens of thousands of dollars worth of labor. I have met so many generous people in the Church, and I'm amazed at their talents. Their lives are an offering to God. As God has richly blessed them with the Holy Spirit, they are now a blessing to others. They are generous givers.

God has named humanity as the stewards of the earth. A steward is someone who manages the affairs of someone else's business. God blessed humanity with this ability. Managing is the one ability that humanity has over all the other species of the animal kingdom. Birds are far more developed to fly, fish are far more developed to swim, lions are much stronger, gazelles are much faster, and squirrels are better climbers. It is arrogant to say that humanity has evolved as a more advanced species, when all other species seem to be superior in so many ways. It isn't a matter of evolution, but rather God has designed and created all species this way. Humanity, as feeble as we are, has been placed in charge. The animal kingdom has so many more dominant

INTRODUCTION

features than humanity, but God placed humanity in charge of the animal kingdom, the fields, the waterways, and the very air we breathe. God has given humanity the ability to co-create. We, like God, can now take the valuable materials of the world to design and make so many amazing inventions. Humanity can use these inventions in the stewardship of enhancing the world, but unfortunately, we can also use them to destroy the world. We have invented machines that run on fossil fuels, only to now have global warming as a result of carbon dioxide emissions. Humanity has invented nuclear energy to power our homes and businesses, but this energy can also be used for mass destruction. As humans, let us see what a gift Creation is to us! Our wealth is having clean air to breathe, fresh water to drink, and soil that produces healthy crops for us to eat.

My mother once taught me a lesson as we were at a picnic site. When the time came for us to leave she said, "Let's walk around the site and pick up whatever garbage is on the ground." As I was picking up garbage, I noticed some that was left by previous visitors. I asked my mother, "Should I pick up other people's garbage?" My mother replied, "Yes, we always want to leave a place better than how we found it." This must be the attitude of every generation. We live and use Creation for our generation, but we must use it in such a way that we are improving it for the generations yet to come.

These were always the grace moments that God shared with me, those little lessons that always seemed so profound. At thirteen years of age, I went canoeing with some friends for a Bible camp adventure. As we paddled along, my friend's canoe capsized. Fortunately, my friend didn't drown, but unfortunately, he lost ten dollars. I felt really bad for him. In 1974, ten dollars was a lot of money for a thirteen year-old. Our camp counselor said, "If you all give him one dollar, then we will all have lost just one dollar." The lesson we learned that day was that we share in each other's gains and losses. When one person suffers, we all suffer; when one person prospers, we all benefit. What seemed like a huge loss for my friend was now a minimal loss for all of us. This is the beauty of the church community; we all are made strong together.

As a pastor, I have met many generous people over the years. They have given willingly and generously to support what is most central in their lives and their faith. As they give, they experience the richness of investing in the Kingdom of God. As they give of their time, talents, and possessions, they are being filled with the richness of God's presence. They know what it is to be members of the kingdom of God on earth as it is in Heaven. As a person loses their life in God, they will gain the fullness of God's presence and will be overflowing with the Holy Spirit.

The familiar cartoon character and ever disgruntled neighbor, Mr. Wilson, bought a personal safe for his home to store his valuables. As he was learning the combination and repeating the numbers to himself, Dennis the Menace was listening. Later that afternoon, Dennis was playing football with his friends. He was playing quarterback and using Mr. Wilson's combination numbers as his cadence before every play. It wasn't long before all the neighborhood kids knew the combination to Mr. Wilson's safe. When Mr. Wilson forgot the numbers to his safe, all the kids were able to remind him what the numbers were. When we lock our godly blessings within ourselves, we die spiritually; when we share our most precious values, we grow spiritually. The Holy Spirit is the combination that unlocks all of Heaven's blessings. The Apostle Paul writes, "In him we have redemption through his blood, the forgiveness of sins, in accordance with the riches of God's grace that he lavished on us with all wisdom and understanding." (Ephesians 1:7-8)

Jesus said, "Do not store up for yourselves treasures on earth, where moth and rust destroy, and where thieves break in and steal. But store up for yourselves treasures in Heaven, where moth and rust do not destroy, and where thieves do not break

INTRODUCTION

in and steal. For where your treasure is, there your heart will be also." (Matthew 6:19-21) We live for a span of time in this life in a world that is subject to decay. When we are generous givers, we are investing in God's kingdom that is eternal. Jesus has given us the eternal kingdom of God. We have been created to invest our lives in Him. "For God so loved the world that he gave his one and only Son, that whoever believes in him shall not perish, but have eternal life." (John 3:16)

You are so valued by God. Jesus died for you. If you were the only person living in the world, Jesus still would have died for you. Your value is priceless to God, even though our world tries to devalue you. God created us, and has now purchased us with the blood of Jesus. We are no longer bound by sin, but freed to be the children of God. "You have been purchased with a price." (1 Corinthians 6:20) God is the creator, and we are the created. God is the owner, and we are the stewards. Most importantly, God is the Heavenly Father, and we are His special children.

> *"Blessed assurance, Jesus is mine!*
> *Oh, what a foretaste of glory divine!*
> *Heir of salvation, purchase of God,*
> *born of his Spirit, washed in his blood."*

As a young boy, I put a quarter in a vending machine that would dispense a plastic capsule with a toy inside it. I was hoping to get one with a Super Ball in it. Instead, I got one that had a girl's ring, so I went home and gave it to my mother. Decades later, I discovered that my mother had kept the trinket ring in her jewelry box for all those years. That ring was of great value to my mother. The values of this world and the values of God are very different. When we come to discover what God values, we now recognize a profound wealth the world will never know.

THE ONION

I HAVE HEARD THIS saying repeated throughout my life: "Give credit where credit is due." I have listened to the displeasure of people who have accomplished something special, only to have somebody else take the credit for it. This explains why inventors will be quick to get a patent, for it won't be long before others will make a claim on the invention and start mass-producing it.

Everything about a beautiful painting will reflect something about the painter. The painter is veiled behind the painting, but yet the painting reveals the painter. It would be an inspiration to meet the painter in person, and spend time in fellowship with him. Creation is God's handprint. Like the painter, God is veiled behind Creation, but yet, God is revealed in every aspect of it. It is amazing that we can come to know God, our Creator in such an intimate way that we can call Him Father.

Regarding Creation, humanity will not give credit to where credit is due. Humanity will not give God credit for creating the universe. When it comes to Creation, we can learn about various theories, but we must ask the most existential question: "What was the first cause of Creation?"

An onion has many layers to it, and we can peel off those layers and be satisfied with a certain layer. When we study theories, we must ask, what layer of the "onion" is this? As we study evolutionary theories, what layer of Creation's "onion" are we examining? We must get right to the core of the onion, and ask the existential question: "How did it all start?" For example, as we study the Big Bang Theory, there are deeper core questions: "Where did the matter come from to begin with?" "What or who caused the big explosion?" "Who was there at the very beginning to give first cause?"

The ancient Greek philosophers also wrestled with these core existential questions. They believed there were four basic elements constituting Creation: earth, wind, fire, and water. They would debate throughout time which element came first, for it was from that element the others came to be. The philosopher Pythagoras believed Creation's order could be credited to the perfect mathematical formulas governing nature from the beginning of time. All of Creation was like musical notes and rhythms that had orchestrated themselves into a symphony. Today, we call such coordination the Laws of Physics.

The Word

The philosopher Heraclitus was also concerned with the existential question, "What is at the core of Creation?" He believed there was a cause prior to the existence of these elements and mathematical laws. He used the word *"logos,"* meaning "the Word," to describe this cause. According to Heraclitus, *logos* was God, the origin of all things.

John's gospel is heavily influenced by Greek thought, and he repeatedly borrows Heraclitus' term when referring to God. He famously uses *logos*, "the Word," to explain that God has come into this world as one of us, as Jesus His incarnate Son. "In the beginning was the Word, and the Word was with God, and the Word was God. He was with God in the beginning. Through him all things were made; without him nothing was made that has been made. In him was life, and that life was the light of men. The light shines in the darkness, but the darkness has not understood it. The Word became flesh and made his dwelling among us. We have seen his glory, the glory of the One and Only, who came from the Father, full of grace and truth." (John 1:1-5, 14)

Forms

Another Greek philosopher, Aristotle, taught that everything comes from a form- a cause that produces an effect. God is the form, the Creator, who produces an effect, Creation. Everything in Creation is an effect of a Creator. To use the very word "Creation" implies that there is a Creator.

If someone were to say to us, "The automobile in your driveway did not have a designer or builder, but rather it just came to be one day," and then continued on to explain its existence by a scientific theory, we would think this person was silly. Creation is far more complex than your automobile; to suggest that it doesn't have a designer or a builder would be nonsense. Creation in all of its facets is an amazing wonder of God, its designer and builder.

Just as automobiles are created from a form in the factory, so we are created in the image of God. What is special about humanity is that we are all created uniquely different, but yet in the image of God. This image has been lost in the fall of humanity, but it is God who redeems us back into the original form through His Son Jesus Christ, the model example for us all. While keeping our uniqueness, we all grow to become more like Jesus, restoring the original form of our creation. The Apostle Paul wrote, "Your attitude should be the same as that of Christ Jesus: Who, being in very form of God, did not consider equality with God something to be grasped, but made himself nothing, taking the very nature of a servant, being made in human likeness. And being found in appearance as a man, he humbled himself and became obedient to death- even death on a cross! Therefore God exalted him to the highest place and gave him the name that is above every name, that at the name of Jesus every knee should bow, in Heaven and on earth and under the earth, and every tongue confess that Jesus Christ is Lord to the glory of God the Father." (Philippians 2:5-11) God created us and has redeemed us in Jesus Christ to the original form of humanity.

A sculptor can look at a stone and see the form of what he wants to create, revealing his masterpiece by cutting away what doesn't belong. That is what God does. He sanctifies us in the Holy Spirit, molding us and making us into His person. Like a sculptor, He cuts away what doesn't belong.

God vs. Science

It is tempting to separate science from God, this way we can claim Creation as our own, rather than it belonging to God. We embrace scientific theories taught from an atheistic perspective, so we are not accountable to God and can live life according to self. Additionally, if a person takes on an atheistic view of life, then they must attempt to explain how this vastly intricate and indescribable Creation came about.

It is important that we reconcile our faith in relationship to God and science. Science isn't studying anything outside of God's Creation. If you think this is the case, then your God is too small. God is not in the corner of the room playing with Play-Dough, but rather is the creator of the Universe and its billions upon billions of galaxies, each containing billions upon billions of stars. As Christians, we embrace science as a godly stewardship that helps us to learn, grow, discover, and develop in the environment of God's creation.

Science is God giving humanity a look into His workshop, and it's interesting to learn about how God does things. When we look at the face of a clock, we would say, "That is time!" When we look at the gears behind the face of the clock we will say,

THE ONION

"That is how time works!" It is very fascinating to see the mechanics of how things operate, and science is taking a look into the mechanics of Creation. Our perceived reality of the Sun is that it rises and sets, but science shows us that the earth rotates while the Sun is stationary. It would be impossible for the Sun to revolve around the earth in 24 hours, so isn't it interesting how God makes the Sun to "rise" and "set"? Our perception is that the earth is flat. After all, people in Australia are not standing upside down. Yet science has shown us that the Earth is round. Isn't it amazing how God does this?

During a visit with a scientist friend (who is both a man of strong faith and author of a textbook that is being used in universities around the world), he taught me about the Second Law of Thermodynamics. He said, "This law states that when something goes from order to chaos, for order to be restored again, it will take something greater than itself to restore that order." In the case of the Big Bang theory, this would suggest that there is order that turns into chaos as the matter explodes and now expands into the Universe. This chaos has been brought back into order. The scientist said, "The only thing that could do this, based on the Second Law of Thermodynamics, is God."

Faith provides insights into the question of "Why?", while science illuminates the question of "How?". Faith and science need to be reconciled and are not to be looked upon as competitors. The Bible's creation stories are not intended to be scientific explanations of *how* God has created, but rather statements of faith that God is the *one* who has created. "In the beginning, God created the heavens and the earth." (Genesis 1:1) The very first verse of the Bible is a confession of faith. As we read the rest of the creation story in Genesis 1, the chapter is written in the form of a hymn. Like any hymn, it contains verses followed by a refrain. This hymn is a faith statement: "All of creation has been created by God." The creation story is the truth of God's inspired Word. It may not be a scientific explanation, but it explains the truth that God has created the heavens and the earth. This is God's way of teaching us; He is at the core of the "onion" when it comes to Creation.

Order

"In the beginning, God created the heavens and the earth. Now the earth was formless and empty, darkness was over the surface of the deep, and the spirit of God was hovering over the waters." (Genesis 1:1-2)

God has given order to Creation through the Laws of Physics. By these laws, all of Creation is orchestrated into amazing clockwork. Everything has to be precisely accurate for Creation to be. For example, the earth is tilted at a 23½ degree axis toward the Sun. If the earth's axis would turn even so slightly, the earth wouldn't have life. The Sun is 93 million miles from the earth. If the earth were nearer or farther away from the sun, the earth could not sustain life. As we study all the many precisions of what has to take place in order for life to exist on earth, we come to appreciate what an amazing creation of God we are living in. God is the mastermind, and we live in a fragile margin of error. If anything alters the balance of Creation ever so slightly, life would cease to exist.

Consider for example how the eye is constructed, that it can receive light, focus on objects, and send the information into the brain for processing. Even the mouth is amazing. It is used to chew food that happens to come from the earth, and have it go through a digestive process that brings nutrients to the body. The mouth is also used for speech. We can take the thoughts of our brains, and send audio messages that enter into the ears of others, where their brains process the information. We can easily take any aspect of Creation and ponder the endless wonderment of it.

Faith Statements

The Apostles' Creed is the faith statement of what we believe as Christians. As the first article of the Apostles' Creed states, "I believe in God the Father almighty, the creator of heaven and earth."

In the Christian church, we sing hymns confessing God as the Creator of all things. One such hymn is, "This is My Father's World."

> *"This is my Father's world, and to my listening ears all nature sings, and round me rings the music of the spheres. This is my Father's world; I rest me in the thought of rocks and trees, of skies and seas; his hand the wonders wrought."*

Another popular hymn is, "How Great Thou Art."

> *"O Lord my God, when I in awesome wonder consider all the works thy hand hath made, I see the stars, I hear the mighty thunder, thy power throughout the universe displayed; Then sings my soul, my Savior God, to thee, how great thou art: How great thou art: Then sings my soul, my Savior God, to thee, how great thou art! How great thou art!"*

Can God create *ex nihilo*, or out of nothing, in an instant? Of course God can. Can God create the universe in six days? Of course God can. Can God create over the course of a long evolutionary period? Of course God can. Maybe the bigger or more important question is, "Is God creating today?" Even though Creation has been in existence for a long time, every spring we see it renewed once again. With the power of the Holy Spirit working in our lives, we see that God is always making us to be a new creation. Apostle Paul writes, "Therefore, if anyone is in Christ, he is a new creation; the old has gone, the new has come!" (2 Corinthians 5:17)

Prayer and Science

I often meet people who are into an either/or understanding of things. I always like to look at the possibility of both. Do we pray or do we look to science? Some will say, "We pray. After all, look at all the miracles that happened in the Bible." Others will say, "We need to turn to science as rational people." We approach these from a stewardship perspective of prayer and science. We pray, because God is engaged in our world and our lives. God makes Himself manifest in all that we think and do. When we pray, we see our faith unfold in God's providential ways. We have also been given the stewardship of Creation, and we all have that special role to play in it.

We must uplift the work of each person, as God uses them as instruments of His amazing work. For example, one day I was driving in the rural countryside when I started having engine trouble. Did I pray or did I go to my mechanic? I was 30 miles away from home, and also from my mechanic's garage. I prayed during the entire drive until I reached the garage. My mechanic shook his head in disbelief asking, "How could you drive this vehicle 30 miles without the engine overheating and having the belt splinter into pieces?" I told him, "I prayed the whole way!" He agreed that there was no logical explanation for this, yet it was a testimony of God working in my life. The mechanic proceeded to replace the engine pulley and belt that runs the water pump, the alternator, and basically the whole mechanical workings of the engine. This is an example of God working through our faithful prayers, and the stewardship of His people.

When we get sick, do we pray or go to the doctor? Much like in the story of the engine, we do pray and ask for God's healing, but we also recognize how God works through the doctor as His steward. God is always working through His spiritual realm and His consecrated physical realm.

Questions

1. Why is it important to look at the core of an onion?
2. What is cause and effect?
3. The Greeks saw the Word as being what?
4. What are forms of creating?
5. How would you describe the wonder of Creation?
6. What are some aspects of Creation that fill you with awe and wonder?
7. How do we reconcile science and God in our understanding of Creation?
8. What scientific theories do you find helpful in understanding Creation?
9. What is your Creation faith statement?
10. How does God bring order out of chaos in Creation, society, and your own personal life?

TWO TREES

THE STORY OF GOD'S people, Israel, begins in Genesis chapter 12, when God calls Abraham to be the father of His great nation. As readers, we sometimes wonder why there are 11 chapters prior to the beginning of the story? These stories give the theological basis of the Bible so that as we read it, we understand why the stories go the way that they do. We learn that God is the Creator, humanity has fallen to sin, God redeems humanity, and God sanctifies us to live as holy people.

Genesis 3:1-24, explains humanity's fall. The characters in this story are: God, Adam, Eve, and a cunning serpent (the Devil). The stage is the Garden of Eden, a place that is flowing with beautiful streams and has an abundance of trees bearing tasty fruit.

In the Garden there are two particularly special trees. One tree is the Tree of Life, representing God. Adam and Eve are to draw their life from this tree. The other is the Tree of the Knowledge of Good and Evil. God forbade Adam and Eve to eat from this tree, for if they did they would be cut off from Him and would die. It is humanity's decision to say, "We can live just fine apart from God, especially now that we have the knowledge and wisdom to function in Creation according to self, rather than Him."

We wonder, why would God place this tree in the Garden of Eden? This seems reckless; if Adam and Eve eat from this tree, it will be disastrous for humanity. God placed this tree for a good reason, because He wants a relationship with us based on love, and not coercion, force, or manipulation. God does not want to be controlling but rather loving. God wants a loving relationship with humanity, just as we want relationships based on love.

The Devil was incarnate in the serpent, who tempted Eve saying, "You will not surely die... For God knows that when you eat of it your eyes will be opened, and you will be like God, knowing good and evil." (Genesis 3:2-3) The fruit looked "good." The fruit tasted "good." The Devil will use "good" to present his evil. The tragedy for Adam and Eve is they now understand good and evil, but have been cut off from their life source. It's like a vine that brings nutrients to the branches- when it is cut, the branches will die.

Humanity's attitude is, "I can live my own life apart from God. I don't need to obey God and have Him tell me how to live my life. I can determine that myself!" Humanity now has its understanding of good and evil. We have life all figured out apart from God. We now have knowledge of good and evil to determine this life. Who needs God? If we want water, we turn on a faucet. If we want light, we turn on a switch. If we need to travel a distance, we get into our automobiles. If there is some area that we are deficient in, we have all kinds of resources to figure things out. The problem lies in the very purpose and intention of our God to live in relationship with Him. We now suffer the consequences of our sin, and we die. All of the king's horses and all of the king's men cannot prevent us from dying. Humanity suffers the pain from its fatal decision.

We may ask, "Did this story really happen or is it a myth?" This story does appear in mythological writings. The Bible is the divinely inspired Word of God. Whether you believe that this story is literally true or figuratively true; it is true. The story is in the Bible, because it best describes the human condition. There is no story in psychology, mythology, or philosophy that can describe the fall of humanity like this one. None of us were there to be an eyewitness to what happened in this story, but we trust in faith that God is teaching the truth through His Word. We ask the question, "Do we see this story happening today?" We see it everyday, as we read about it in the newspapers, and watch it on the television news broadcasts. Did we see the story of Adam and Eve happening in our parent's generation? Yes, of course. Did we see the story happening in our grandparent's generation? Yes, of course. As we read throughout the history of humanity, we can see the story of Adam and Eve repeating. We can conclude that humanity's first parents suffered from temptation and the consequential fall.

The Tree of Knowledge of Good and Evil

Humanity draws from the Tree of Knowledge of Good and Evil, and with this knowledge we now determine what is good and evil based on our judgment of it. When we draw life from the Tree of Knowledge of Good and Evil, we believe that we have the knowledge of salvation based on our goodness. We believe that we are saved by our goodness, and that we are the standard or gauge of how goodness is measured, putting ourselves in the place to judge others. As a humanity we have this strong sense that we are saved by the good works that we merit.

Goodness varies from person to person. My definition of "good" will be different from the next person's definition of "good". We must learn that God's definition of goodness is very different from humanity's. Jesus said, "Only God is good." (Matthew 19:17) I can say, "There is a good person, or there is a bad person." It doesn't matter what I think, for it is only God who can judge the goodness of a person. We have God's goodness for salvation. God's goodness is His love and grace in Jesus who saves us. The Apostle Paul writes, "My grace is sufficient for you, for my power is made perfect in weakness." (2 Corinthians 12:9)

The fruit of this tree has been appealing to humanity all the way back to our first parents Adam and Eve. We want to pick the fruits of our own wisdom, strength, and goodness from this tree. Instead of bringing the appealing taste of fullness in life, it only brings, emptiness, despair, and death. Only God can satisfy the inner spiritual longings of the human heart.

Paganism

Paganism is worshipping a god that we have created in our image. Paganism is taking all of what we think is good and righteous, putting it in the melting pot of our brain, and making an idol of it. In Paganism, god will differ from person-to-person, since god is an individual creation. Many Pagans will have some Christian principles embedded in their thinking, since many Pagans have grown up in Christianity.

Paganism is self-serving. It emphasizes the individual, and it is a religion of convenience. There is very little sacrifice, and it fits perfectly to the individual's lifestyle. Pagans have no need of Jesus, since they believe salvation is based on their own goodness and intellectual understanding. Paganism is not to be confused with Christianity, which bases its teachings on salvation in Jesus alone.

The Tree of Life

What would life look like if Adam and Eve had not fallen to sin? We can only imagine. Apostle John in Revelation 21:3-4, "And I heard a loud voice from the throne saying, 'Now the dwelling of God is with men, and he will live with them. They will be his people, and God himself will be with them and be their God. He will wipe every tear from their eyes. There will be no more death or mourning or crying or pain, for the old things have passed away."

The Tree of Life, being Jesus, has been stripped of its glory. Jesus was crucified and rose from the dead. As He offers His life to us, life with God that was lost has now been redeemed. We can be restored in the image of God.

Jesus said, "I am the vine; you are the branches. If a man remains in me and I in him, he will bear much fruit; apart from me you can do nothing." (John 15:5) Jesus is the vine that brings life to the branches. Notice Jesus said, "branches", meaning plural. It is by love that God brings us into fellowship with Him, and it is by His love that we come together to be the Church. We draw eternal life from the Tree of Life, and our wisdom is a Heavenly one. God allows us to bear fruit, the spiritual virtues that He desires for our life. They go contrary to the sinful desires of our heart.

As the Apostle Paul writes, "The acts of the sinful nature are obvious: sexual immorality, impurity and debauchery, idolatry and witchcraft; hatred, discord, jealousy, fits of rage, selfish ambition dissensions, factions and envy; drunkenness, orgies, and the like. I warn you, as I did before, that those who live like this will not inherit the kingdom of God. But the fruit of the Spirit is love, joy, peace, patience, kindness, goodness, faithfulness, gentleness and self-control. Against such things there is no law. Those who belong to Christ Jesus have crucified the sinful nature with its passions and desires."(Galatians 5:19-24)

Even though humanity has knowledge of good and evil, the consequence of being cut off from God produces the fruit of the flesh and death. When we repent of our sinful life and receive the life of Jesus, we produce the spiritual fruit and virtues that only God can produce in us.

Stewards

God has called us to be the stewards of Creation. A steward is someone who manages what belongs to someone else. In the fall, humanity now makes claim to be the owner of God's Creation. Humanity has put itself in a place where it doesn't belong.

As we worship God and receive His salvation, we repent of arrogant Pagan attitudes. We are brought back into the proper relationship with God, remembering that He is the Creator and we are the created. God is the owner and we are the stewards. God is the Heavenly Father, and we are His children. As we draw life from the Tree of Life, we keep this perspective.

The beginning of the Bible describes the two trees, and we hear of them again at the end of the Bible as we read in Revelation 22:1-3, "Then the angel showed me the river of the water of life, as clear as crystal, flowing from the throne of God and of the Lamb down the middle of the great street of the city. On each side of the river stood the Tree of Life, bearing twelve crops of fruit, yielding its fruit every month. And the leaves of the tree are for the healing of the nations." Humanity has been restored, and the door of the eternal paradise that once was closed has now been reopened.

The two trees are ever present before us, and we always have the choice as to where we will draw life. Moses addressed the people as he led them out of Egypt through the Red Sea, for forty years in the wilderness, and to the Jordan River. As he was preparing to pass his leadership to Joshua before entering into the Promised Land he said, "This day I call Heaven and Earth as witnesses against you that I have set before you life and death, blessing and curses. Now choose life, so that you and your children may live and that you may love the Lord your God, listen to his voice, and hold fast to him. For the Lord is your life, and he will give you many years in the land he swore to give to your fathers, Abraham, Isaac, and Jacob." (Deuteronomy 30:19-20)

Draw life from the Tree of life. This way you will live in fellowship with God, your Heavenly Father.

Because of humanity's fall to sin, it is our desire to be God. We work to build our little empires, or in the case of atrocious leaders in history, the desire to rule all the nations. This causes ruthless competition, wars, oppression, and heinous acts upon humanity. As we draw from the Tree of Life, we now desire to be imitators of God, following in the humble example of Jesus who was the King dying on the tree for our sins. One side of the cross represents the tree of Knowledge of Good and Evil. It is for this reason that Jesus suffered and died on that side of the cross. The other side is empty, representing the forgiveness and the resurrection we have in Jesus Christ. It is by coming to the cross of Christ that we confess our sins of desiring to be God, while the other side represents the forgiveness of our sins, and the desire to be imitators of God in Christ Jesus. "Be imitators of God, therefore, as dearly loved children and live a life of love, just as Christ loved us and gave himself up for us as a fragrant offering and sacrifice to God." (Ephesians 5:1-2)

Questions

1. What is the purpose of the first 11 chapters of the Bible?
2. What are the two trees, and why are they in the Garden of Eden?
3. How do you see the story of the fall to sin truth?
4. How do we draw life from the Tree of Good and Evil?
5. What is humanity's attitude toward God since the fall?
6. What is Paganism?
7. What is appealing about Paganism?
8. Who is the Tree of Life?
9. What is the godly perspective of a steward?
10. What is it now to live in the image of God?

SACRAMENTAL GOD

THE WORD "SACRAMENT" COMES from the root word "sacred," meaning holy and set apart for the purposes of God. Another word with this root is "sacrifice." Sacrifice is our giving something to God, while sacrament is God giving something to us. The great sacrifice that God has made for humanity is giving His Son, Jesus Christ who died for us. God uses the very elements of His Creation as vehicles of this amazing grace.

God is Holy. Because of this, we cannot catch, contain, control, or possess God. God is beyond our reason, strength, and intellectual comprehension. He is veiled in Creation and holiness, and reveals Himself through His Son, Jesus Christ.

So often we hear people say, "We want to see God!" We look for God in supernatural events, while we think that God is apart from the natural. People want to see a miracle. God does work miracles, but for the most part, God works sacramentally in and through the natural order of His Creation. We need to recognize this understanding. All of Creation is a blessing, and God works in the blessedness of the Creation. Ultimately, God is working to bring unity in all of Creation, in Heaven and Earth through Jesus.

God works through His Word. "In the beginning was the Word, and the Word was with God, and the Word was God. He was with God in the beginning...The Word became flesh and made his dwelling among us." (John 1:1-3, 14) God does not come as an extra-terrestrial, but rather as one of us. He relates to us in every way.

God takes the elements of Creation to be the vehicles of His grace. The salvation life of Jesus is given in our baptisms, as God links life-giving water with His Word. Jesus also takes the bread and says, "This is my body", and the wine saying, "This is my blood." God works sacramentally, meaning through the very common elements of His Creation, to bring us salvation.

Stewards of the Earth

"The Lord God took the man and put him in the Garden of Eden to work it and take care of it." (Genesis 2:15) God created the heavens and the earth. God the Father spoke His Word and all of Creation came together. God the Son, was in the beginning as the Word, and God the Holy Spirit was moving over the face of the earth, bringing order to Creation. The triune God was working in perfect harmony bringing Creation to life.

All of Creation has its purpose. The bees understand their work in the hive, the ants have their work in their mound, and beavers work tirelessly building their homes. The polar bear is the king of the ice, while the lion is the king of the jungle. They know how to take care of their habitats.

God has given humanity the special calling of being the stewards of the earth. We are to live in harmony with God, and all of Creation. A steward is the manager of what belongs to someone else. I have known many people who have been in the top role of being the manager, but even at that, the manager is not the owner.

Do you value what belongs to someone else more than what belongs to yourself? I have heard people say, "People do not respect the property of others as much as they value their own." It should be the opposite. When someone loans something to us, we should treat it with the utmost respect. As for Creation, we are to manage it in such a way that we leave it in better shape than when we found it.

Sin and Separation

As a result of the fall, humanity isn't interested in being the steward to have dominion over the earth, instead humanity wants to be the owner and have dominance over Creation. Humanity's attitude toward Creation is one of consumption, rather than preservation for the generations to come.

We do not want God to be part of what we now interpret as being our Creation. We are the owner, and God is the trespasser. As humanity, we have taken God out of the world. We have chosen different values. In public places, there is a complete intolerance of God's presence. We have knocked God out of it. We don't want prayer in schools, nor do we want the Ten Commandments in courtrooms. We have legislated laws to keep God out. Recently, I had a speaking engagement in a public place where they didn't want me to use the word "chastity" because the people felt it had Christian connotations.

At what point are living trees and plants no longer allowed on public property? After all, God created them. Will we settle for artificial trees and plants in public places? People can become so frustrated living in God's Creation, that we try to create a world that is artificial.

We have been created in the image of God, so we too have the ability to design and create. New York City is an empire that is built of cement and asphalt. As I have done mission work at an inner city church, I am amazed at how the people value their little green spaces. They were so proud to show me their little flower gardens that they were able to create. During my time there, I met a green space architect. As I was working with a crew to renovate the church's courtyard, I accidently stepped on a plant. I thought the green space architect was going to have a stroke. As someone who grew up in a small town in Wisconsin, this surprised me. We were surrounded by so much vegetation that we took it for granted, but for these New Yorkers, plant life was so special that stepping on a small plant was devastating.

Central Park in New York City is a large green space, but one of the things that I noticed while sitting on a park bench was the infestation of rats. Snakes may seem creepy and not very cuddly, but they do keep the rodent population down. Central Park could use some snakes. All species were created by God to keep the world's ecosystem in a proper balance.

As humans, we continue to destroy precious animal habitat. Some animal species are now extinct, while others are on the endangered species list. All things live within a small margin of error. If one species goes extinct, that is a bad sign for the human race as members of the animal kingdom. We are created in the image of God, and have been given a special place as God's people; but we still live in this environment. It is the life support system for all living things.

Jesus told a parable, "A man planted a vineyard, rented it to some farmers and went away for a long time. At harvest time he sent a servant to the tenants so they would give him some of the fruit of the vineyard. But the tenants beat him and sent him away empty-handed. He sent another servant, but they also beat that one and treated him shamefully and sent him away empty-handed. He sent still a third, and they wounded him, and threw him out. Then the owner of the vineyard said, 'What shall I do? I will send my son, whom I love, perhaps they will respect him.' But when the tenants saw him, they talked the matter over. 'This is the heir,' they said, 'Let's kill him, and the inheritance will be ours.' So they threw him out of the vineyard and killed him. What then, will the owner of the vineyard do to them? He will come and kill those tenants and give the vineyard to others."

(Luke 20:9-16) Humanity is always working to take ownership of what belongs to God. God sent His Son, Jesus, into the world, and humanity thought that by killing Him they would have ownership over Creation. This would certainly solidify the original sin of their parents, Adam and Eve. Instead, God has purchased again what belonged to Him originally.

A boy made a boat with a beautiful knife he had gotten for his birthday. He took the boat and sailed it on a small pond in his community. He would release the boat into the pond, and then run to the other side to meet it. One day as he was doing this, he reached the other side of the lake and found his boat in the hands of a bully. The boy said to the bully, "Please give me my boat back!" The bully replied, "This is my boat!" The boy insisted, "No it isn't! I made it with my knife." The bully looked at the knife and said, "You can have your boat back if you give me your knife." The boy gave the bully his knife. As the boy walked home he said to his boat, "You are twice mine! First I made you, and now I have purchased you back with my knife." This is what God has done. He first made us, and has now purchased us back with the price of His Son. "He was in the world, and though the world was made through him, the world did not recognize him. He came to that which was his own, but his own did not receive him. Yet to all who received him, to those who believed in his name, he gave the right to become children of God." (John 1:10-11) In Jesus there is transformation and new life. He has reconciled us, and we can live in harmony with God, the Father. It is also important to be reconciled with all Creation, and to live in a peaceful harmony.

The Elements

As we look at the world today, we see that the air, water, and ground have been contaminated with pollution. The carbon dioxide we emit into the air has produced a greenhouse effect that threatens our very existence. The chemicals that we apply to our soil and plants have contaminated the most basic grains that we eat, so that many people now have reactions to these products. We are draining our earth of its minerals, oil, and water.

The good news is, humanity is starting to use the basic elements of the earth to create renewable energies. There are solar farms that harness the power of the sun, wind farms harnessing the power of the wind, hydro-dams harnessing the power of water, and more and more conservation methods have been developed to preserve the soil. All of these measures will make for a healthier earth.

It is important for us to conserve water, turn off electrical appliances when not using them, recycle our disposables, and to implement renewable energy technology as it becomes available. It is also important to use biodegradable materials rather than plastics.

Other ways that we can conserve is by riding bikes or walking to places, carpooling, and taking public transportation. We may sometimes feel powerless to make changes in our world, but if everyone would work on doing the little things, this will make a big impact on environmental preservation.

Sacramental People

As God came into this world, He uses the very natural resources that He has created to bring forth His purposes for creation and salvation. God has called us to be sacramental people too. It is God's desire for us to live in harmony with Creation. We too are to be holy, for God wants us to be holy as He is holy. (1 Peter 1:16) When we live holy lives, we desire to live in relationship with God the Father, our Creator, and to be faithful in the special calling of being stewards of the earth.

God has made Himself sacramental in that He became incarnate in His Son, Jesus Christ. God became human flesh, one of us. God has identified with humanity in all points. Jesus is both fully God and fully human. This point came to a culminating moment when Jesus died for our sins. God took our transgressions upon Himself as the perfect Lamb of God in order to take away the sins of the world. Jesus is the complete savior; we need nothing more. Jesus fully satisfies the expectations that God has for righteousness.

God continues to make Himself incarnate in Jesus through the hearing of His Word, as well as in the earthly elements of water through holy baptism, and in the bread and wine during holy communion. These are the means of God's grace; it is in these ways that God offers the salvation life of Jesus to humanity.

Questions

1. Why can't God be contained?
2. How do you look for God in the natural?
3. How do all created things fulfill a godly purpose?
4. How is humanity working contrary to its calling as stewards of Creation and life?
5. Are you more intrigued by soil and water, or concrete and asphalt?
6. Do you know of any animals that are on the endangered species list?
7. How does the parable of the tenants explain humanity's attitude toward God?
8. What is the purchase of God?
9. What can we do to be better stewards?
10. How is God sacramental for us?

100%

I KNEW A GIRLS basketball coach who had built a strong, winning program. His teams were perennial conference champions, and also won some state basketball championships. These players gave a lot of reason for their fans to cheer. On a summer's day, one of the players was tragically killed in a car accident. As I sat with the grieving coach at the hospital he said, "My players give me 100%. They give me everything they've got!" The love that this coach had for his players was very evident, and the players showed their appreciation for him in return, as they would give him their best effort.

The Widow's Mite

As we read in Luke 21:1-4, "As he looked up, Jesus saw the rich putting their gifts into the temple treasury. He also saw a poor widow put in two very small copper coins. 'I tell you the truth.' He said, 'this poor widow has put in more than all the others. All these people gave their gifts out of their wealth; but she out of her poverty put in all she had to live on.'" It was the time of the Passover festival. People were coming to the temple to give their temple taxes. This became a big production, as the wealthy people were coming to put on a show of giving large sums of money. The temple treasury was pleased with this, for it would cover all their operating expenses. This widow came unnoticed by the crowd and gave two copper coins. It was an insignificant amount, but yet in proportion to what she had, she gave 100%. Who is this widow? The widow is Jesus. Jesus, who had nothing of earthly value in this world and life, gave everything he had; he gave his life. Jesus gave 100% of Himself to save the whole world.

Heavenly Fragrance

We hear another story from John 12:1-3, "Six days before the Passover, Jesus arrived at Bethany, where Lazarus lived, whom Jesus had raised from the dead. Here a dinner was given in Jesus' honor. Martha served, while Lazarus was among those reclining at the table with him. Then Mary took about a pint of pure spikenard, an expensive perfume. She poured it on Jesus' feet and wiped his feet with her hair, and the house was filled with the fragrance of the perfume." As Mary and Martha were friends of Jesus, they would open their home to him and show him kind hospitality. They also had a brother named Lazarus, who Jesus raised from the dead. As Mary anointed Jesus' feet with such an expensive perfume, it cost her everything she had. This didn't matter because Jesus was of priceless worth to Mary. This is Mary's expression of love to Jesus, "You are my greatest value in life!"

Normally kings, prophets, and priests would be anointed on the head. Jesus was all of these, but His feet were anointed rather than His head. This is because Jesus is the Messiah, the suffering servant who would die for humanity's sins. The perfume that Jesus was anointed with is Heaven's scent. It lingers throughout eternity.

The Apostle Paul writes, "But thanks be to God, who always leads us in triumphal procession in Christ and through us spreads everywhere the fragrance of the knowledge of him. For we are to

God the aroma of Christ among those who are being saved and those who are perishing." (2 Corinthians 2:14-15)

As I was doing missionary work in Russia, the senior pastor of the church where I was working read the previous passage to his congregation and encouraged them to be this sweet fragrance to the community as they went about their good works. During my trip I had the chance to visit the church's rehabilitation center, a dairy farm where the residents would milk cows. When I returned to the hotel at the end of my tour, my roommate was using the restroom. I could smell a strong odor. The odor was still very potent after some time, and I realized it did not come from the restroom after all but was manure on my shoes. As we live life, we don't want to stink by mistreating people. Instead, we want to show kindness, especially to the poor whom Jesus called us to serve.

I knew a wealthy man who would occasionally stop by the church and leave a nice check to support our ministry and mission work. Traces of his expensive signature cologne always lingered even an hour after he'd left my office. Like this man's generosity and cologne, we want the good works that we do in the name of Jesus to have a lingering fragrance that people will always remember.

What do we Give?

God has given 100% of his person to us, so what do we give in return? Jesus said, "If anyone would come after me, he must deny himself and take up his cross and follow me." (Matthew 16:24) What God wants from all of us is a special relationship. He wants us fully committed. I'm reminded of the story of a man who was preparing for his baptismal ceremony in a lake. The pastor said, "Your wallet is in your back pocket, don't you want to take it out?" The man chuckled in reply, "No, I think that needs to be baptized too." He understood that God doesn't want partial commitments, nor for us to compartmentalize life.

We are to give 100% of our person to the Lord, so when the offering plate comes by, do we jump into it? When I was a child in the late 1960s and early '70s, I loved to go sledding with my friends. In that era we had sleds with runners on them, but one winter there came a new sledding phenomenon: the invention of aluminum saucers. I still remember the bracing thrill of sitting in the saucer and flying down the hill. Initially, this felt reckless and out of control, but we soon learned to steer them by leaning. This is my personal visual of "being in the offering plate." When we first give our lives to the Lord it seems like a reckless step of faith, but as we follow Him we develop a trusting relationship.

As far as giving financially to Jesus' Church, we give out of a loving desire for Him. Because we come from a place of thankfulness for what the Lord has already provided us, we give back a portion of our income. People may complain about giving to the Church, but yet are generous to what they do value in this world and life. We do give to the priorities we believe in. Our checkbooks are statements of faith; they will always tell what is of highest value.

Tithing

A wonderful goal to have in our giving is to tithe, meaning giving 10% of our earnings to the work of our Lord. "A tithe of everything from the land, whether grain from the soil or fruit from the trees, belongs to the Lord; it is holy to the Lord. If a man redeems any of his tithe, he must add a fifth of the value to it. The entire tithe of the herd and flock-every tenth animal that passes under the shepherd's rod-will be holy to the Lord. He must not pick out the good from the bad or make any substitution. If he does make a substitution, both the animal and its substitute become holy and cannot be redeemed." (Leviticus 27:30-33)

Also as we read from Malachi 3:8-10, "Will a man rob God? Yet you rob me. But you ask, 'How do we rob you?' 'In tithes and offerings. You are under a curse-the whole nation of you- because you are robbing me. Bring the whole tithe into the storehouse, that there may be food in my house. Test me in this,' says the Lord Almighty, 'and see if I will not throw open the floodgates of heaven and pour out so much blessing that you will not have room enough for it.'"

I was 16 when my brother asked me if I tithed. I didn't have any idea what he was talking about. He told me that it was a Biblical principle, so I decided to try it. I would work at my high school job all day and earn $10, then giving $1 as my tithe to my church. I didn't really know what the church did with it, nor did I care since it was my offering. It was my offering that I gave to God, and God knew my heart's intention. I didn't know if they buried the offerings or perhaps just burned them out back. With time I learned about all of the important ministries and missions the offerings went to support, and tithing became my lifelong practice. I don't do it in hopes of having God bless me with more financial resources, nor do I do it to brag and impress other people. I do it simply because I love the Lord, and I want to give to the cause that I believe in.

I have heard many testimonies from people who committed to tithing and saw their lives completely change. God blessed them in so many ways. For example, one person had a failing business but still prioritized tithing. God kept blessing him more and more until his business grew to be the second most profitable in his county. I have also heard of churches that started tithing their offerings to the greater work of the Church, and their offerings increased immensely. When we can be trusted with a little, then God increases that trust with more. We are not to test the Lord our God, except for that one principle and that is tithing. The best way to experience the blessedness of tithing is to take a step of faith and just do it!

Generous Giving

Some people make tithing their goal, but work toward it in incremental steps. They begin by giving 1%, and the next year they increase by a percentage until they eventually reach the goal of giving 10%. I knew one young family man who was working hard just to make ends meet. One day a member of the church encouraged him to make an annual pledge, but he said he couldn't afford it. The church member said, "Could you give 1% of your income?" The man said, "No", but then calculated what 1% would be. He said, "I spend more than that on cigarettes, so yes I will." Every year he increased his giving to where he eventually gave 13%. I even knew a bishop who double tithed, giving 20% to the Lord. He said, "In all of my years I have not met an ex-tither, but I have met many blessed tithers."

I'm reminded of one little boy who was so honored to collect the offering on Sunday morning. When he finished passing the offering plate from row to row, he ran enthusiastically with the filled plate to the altar. In his excitement, he tripped and fell, spilling the offerings all over the altar. We must remember that Jesus' blood was spilled all over the world. It is salvation for the world, and to each one of us. As we give our offerings, they too are spilled all over the world, the world being God's altar. These are offerings that support the work of Jesus' Church throughout the world. Just as a dairy farmer wants to see his bulk tank overflowing with milk, so God wants His offering plates to overflow with the offerings of His people.

Questions
1. What does giving 100% mean to you?
2. What did the widow give? What do you think of this story?
3. Who is the widow?
4. When are you a fragrance of God?
5. What is the nature of God's fragrance?
6. What does Mary's fragrance represent?
7. Was the perfume a waste of money?
8. What do you value as your fragrance?
9. Is giving a tithe a reckless or faithful step?
10. What does Jesus want us to give?

THE HOLY SPIRIT & THE CHURCH

Having the Holy Spirit is the impetus of being a Christian. The Holy Spirit gives the power to transform lives, and the passion to be God's people. An automobile that does not have gasoline in its tank cannot be moved, just as a Christian without the Holy Spirit will not be going anywhere.

The Work of the Holy Spirit

John 14 & 16 provides us with helpful insight on the Holy Spirit. Jesus said, "Do not let your hearts be troubled. Trust in God; trust also in me. In my Father's house are many rooms; if it were not so, I would have told you. I am going there to prepare a place for you." (John 14:1-2) Jesus gives the promise of preparing a place for us in Heaven. We hold this precious promise. Jesus then informs the disciples that He will soon be leaving. They are deeply grieved by this news and feel like orphaned children. Jesus reassures them, "But I tell you the truth. It is for your good that I am going away. Unless I go away, the Counselor will not come to you, but if I go, I will send him to you." (John 16:7)

The Counselor Jesus speaks of is the Holy Spirit. This is the omnipresence of God that dwells in the believers.

Jesus made the promise, "And surely I am with you always, to the very end of the age." (Matthews 28:20) How can Jesus promise to be with us while informing us that he is leaving? How is this possible? It is made possible by the coming of the Holy Spirit. God's Kingdom is being established on Earth as it is in Heaven.

People often wonder where Heaven is. It's part of our human nature to want to get there by our own efforts. Just as the story of the Tower of Babel in Genesis 11 describes, the people were attempting to build a tower tall enough to reach Heaven. Even when astronauts have pierced through the Earth's atmosphere and ascended into space, people asked, "Where is Heaven? Jesus? The angels?" The question continues to be asked as space probes and powerful telescopes have been able to look deeper into the universe. My hunch is that Heaven is nowhere to be found in this universe. We could go to the farthest galaxies, and we would not find Heaven. The important point to remember is that God knows where Heaven is. Heaven isn't a place that we discover by our own efforts, but rather it has come to us in Jesus. Jesus said, "The Kingdom of God does not come with your careful observation, nor will people say, 'Here it is,' or 'There it is,' because the kingdom of God is within you." (Mark 12:34)

It is God's plan to establish his kingdom on earth in the believers' hearts and make them the holy temple of God. So, how do we receive the Holy Spirit? In Luke 11, Jesus gives His instruction on prayer. In verse 13 Jesus said, "If you then, though you are evil, know how to give good gifts to your children, how much more will your Father in Heaven give the Holy Spirit to those who ask Him?"

As we read in John 16:7-11, the Holy Spirit will do three things. The first is that He will convict us of our sins. This is not easy for us, because we get defensive. We will want to make the strong argument for innocence, but when we examine ourselves and are honest, we confess our sins. When we have been convicted of our sins, the second thing the Holy Spirit does is convince us that Jesus is the savior who died for our sins. It is in Him that we have forgiveness and receive the free gift of salvation. The third thing the Holy Spirit does is sanctify us in the truth. Sanctify means, "to be made holy, set apart for the purposes of God." To be sanctified means that we grow in our relationship with God, the Father. We grow in our understanding of the truth of God in relationship to Him, the world, and our lives. It is this truth that sets us free to be the people of God, and to gain spiritual insight for our lives. Not that we ever become perfect in this life, but we make it our aim to grow in the likeness of Jesus every day. One day, when we enter eternal life, we no longer will suffer with sin, but will be made in the perfect likeness of Jesus. We shouldn't worry about where Heaven is, or what it will be like. Its spiritual significance is being in relationship with God, the Father now and forever.

Holy Life and Transformation

The Apostle Paul writes, "I have been crucified in Christ, it is no longer I who lives, but it is Christ who lives within me." (Galatians 2:20) We are filled with the salvation life of God. The Holy Spirit dwells within each one of us.

Again Paul writes, "Therefore, I urge you brothers, in view of God's mercy, to offer your bodies as living sacrifices holy and pleasing to God- this is your spiritual act of worship. Do not conform any longer to the pattern of this world, but be transformed by the renewing of your mind. Then you will be able to test and approve what God's will is- His good, pleasing, and perfect will." (Romans 12:1-2) As God transforms us from the inside out, He remakes and molds us more and more into the likeness of Jesus Christ.

There is behavioral psychology that will work to modify our behavior, by using methods of negative and positive reinforcements, cognitive therapy, and classical conditioning. It is a training to help us to do right, and to refrain from doing wrong. Even though such methods may be helpful, they do not change the inward attitude of a person's will and desires. We may desire to harm another person, but since we have been trained to learn the consequences we refrain from doing this action. Still, it doesn't change the ill-felt intentions toward others. The Holy Spirit transforms us to where we no longer desire to harm anyone, but rather to reach out in love. The Holy Spirit gives us the transforming power to turn hate into love, greed into generosity, war into peace, anger into patience, and harm into protection.

The Apostles' Creed is a basic confession of what Christians believe. We believe in one God, in three persons: Father, Son, and Holy Spirit. There are three articles of the Apostles Creed. The first article is, "I believe in God the Father." The second article is, "I believe in God the Son." The third article is, "I believe in God the Holy Spirit." In his explanation of the third article, Martin Luther states, "But the Holy Spirit has called me through the Gospel, enlightened me with his gifts, and sanctified and kept me in the true faith. In the same way he calls, gathers, enlightens, and sanctifies the whole Christian church on earth." In other words, he says the Holy Spirit gathers us to be the Church. The Church is the product of the Holy Spirit. This is God's kingdom on Earth as it is in Heaven. To deny the Church is to deny the Holy Spirit. This grieves the Holy Spirit. "And do not grieve the Holy Spirit of God, with whom you were sealed for the day of redemption." (Ephesians 5:30)

Bonded in Love

Jesus said, "'Love the Lord your God with all your heart and with all your soul and with all your mind. This is the first and greatest commandment. And the second is like it: Love your neighbor as yourself.'" (Matthew 22:37-39) The bonds that are the strongest are the spiritual ones, they go to the very depth and inner being of our person. As God has loved us, we are now called to love one another. First and foremost, the Church is to be a loving church. If the Church only has that ingredient, it will be strong. Apostle Paul writes, "If I speak in the tongues of men and of angels, but have not love, I am only a resounding gong or a clanging cymbal." (1 Corinthians 13:1) We can be the most talented people in the world, but if we have no love then we will not be edifying the Church; if anything we will be using our talent to bring others down. We can be arrogant, narcissistic, critical, and condescending to others. Our talent will be like a wrecking ball. It is important that we allow the love of Christ Jesus to dwell in our lives. Love is a verb, rather than a feeling. Even if we do not have an affinity toward someone, it is always important to love others through our words and actions.

The Family of God

The Church is bonded in the love of God. We are so bonded that we call God "father," and we call fellow members "brothers and sisters in Jesus Christ." I know there are many people who have been abused by their earthly fathers, and I know families where siblings are estranged. We must remember that God is a loving father, and His desire for His church is to be bonded in His love. Apostle Paul writes, "For this reason I kneel before the Father, from whom his whole family in heaven and on earth derives its name. I pray that out of his glorious riches he may strengthen you with power through his spirit in your inner being, so that Christ may dwell in your hearts through faith." (Ephesians 3:14-17) The Church has to come together to worship the Lord, and bring glory to His name, as we work together for His purposes, edifying the church.

The role that we have in our nuclear family is often the role that we have in the Church. For example, if we were a leader in our family, then we generally will be a leader in the Church. If we were the comforter of the family, we will likely be a comforter in the Church. Likewise, if we are the problem solver in our family, then that will be our role. God has blessed us with a family, so that we can be nurtured in an intimate love and mature into confident and well-adjusted people. We carry this healthy mindset with us as we assume our roles as members of the Church.

The Body of Christ

Apostle Paul states, "Just as each of us has one body with many members, and these members do not all have the same function, so in Christ we who are many form one body, and each member belongs to all the others." (Romans 12:4-5) Paul gives a simple illustration that helps us to understand the Church; it is like a body with its many individual parts working toward one cause. The right hand is very different from the left ear, but yet they work together to support the whole. If the right hand were detached from our body, we may say, "It is a good right hand." Yet, what good would it be doing? If the right hand could speak and say, "I can be a good right hand apart from the body," that would be arrogance. Could we live without our right hand? We probably could, but wouldn't it be better for us to have our right hand? If someone says, "I can be a good Christian apart from the body," that too would be arrogance. Together we are stronger. Jesus said, "Blessed are the poor in spirit, for theirs is the kingdom of heaven." (Matthew 5:3) The poor in spirit are those who recognize they cannot save themselves by their own goodness, but rather come to salvation in Jesus Christ. They are filled with the Holy Spirit.

Jesus Christ is the head of the Church, the body of Christ. We always have to keep this focus. We receive our leadership from Jesus, and we find our unity in Him. When the Church is unified in Jesus, then we can celebrate the diversity of its members. We no longer see others as a threat, nor are we jealous of their abilities. Instead, we now celebrate each other's gifts and we always use them for His glory and service. We can embrace each other even though we may be of a different race, sex, or political persuasion. One person may be gifted in music, while another in teaching, and yet another in administration. We must remember that we are stronger together. For example, a church call committee interviewing a pastor friend asked, "Are you musical?" He replied, "No, but my wife is an accomplished organist and can direct a choir." My friend was chosen for the position. He knew that he couldn't cover everything alone, but by humbly acknowledging his personal weakness and showcasing his wife's talent instead, he became an even stronger candidate. This is the attitude the Church has. We have the abilities and resources to accomplish all that God has called us to do. As individuals we may not get very far, but together we can do all things!

We may strive to live as independent people, more often we find ourselves being dependent. We are to be interdependent, where we rely on each other to be the Church. Where we are weak, we are made strong, because we share the talents that work for the sake of the whole.

Some people will say, "Christians are people who need a crutch." To these people I would ask, "Don't you ever need a doctor or a plumber? How about a grocer or mechanic? Do you ever need comfort or to be loved?" A person like this will probably say, "And I will never need a mortician because I will never die!" The reality is, we need each other. We share our mutual talents for the strength and well-being of the Church.

"Trust in the Lord with all your heart and lean not on your own understanding. In all your ways acknowledge him, and he will make your paths straight." (Proverbs 3:5-6) We are to trust and lean on God, and as we do, we lean on each other. The Apostle Peter wrote, "The stone the builders rejected has become the capstone." (1 Peter 2:7) A capstone was the stone that arches of a doorway would lean on. If we were to see ourselves as being arches of a doorway, we are all leaning on Jesus, and being a strong church on earth.

Talents

The Apostle Peter writes, "Like good stewards of the manifold grace of God, serve one another with whatever gift each of you has received." (1 Peter 4:10) God has blessed each person with at least one talent to be developed and used in the service of the Church.

The Apostle Paul mentions some of the talents that people will have to share in their churches, "We have different gifts according to the grace given us. If a man's gift is prophesying, let him use it in proportion to his faith. If it is serving, let him serve; if it is teaching, let him teach; if it is encouraging, let him encourage; if it is contributing to the needs of others, let him give generously; if it is leadership, let him govern diligently; if it is showing mercy, let him do it cheerfully." (Romans 12:6-8)

Prophesying is the gift to speak God's Word. Public speaking is known to be most people's greatest fear. Who has enough courage to speak out? The prophet Jeremiah said, "His word is in my heart like a fire, a fire shut up in my bones." (Jeremiah 20:9) The prophet Isaiah said, "Then one of the seraphs flew to me with a live coal in his hand, which he had taken with tongs from the altar. With it he touched my mouth and said, 'See, this has touched your lips; your guilt is taken away and your sin atoned for.'" (Isaiah 6:6-7) The prophet Ezekiel ate the Word and said it was sweet, "Then he said to me, 'Son of man, eat this scroll I am giving you and fill your stomach with it.' So I ate it, and it tasted as sweet as honey in my mouth." (Ezekiel 3:3) With all of these prophets, it was God who gave the ability to speak his Word with bold confidence. God gives the preacher the ability to speak his Word. A prophet speaks God's Word in the present, but also has a message for the future. Prophecy is not fortune-telling, but rather forth-telling. Just as a good historian can tell the events of the past, the prophet can share the events of the future. The prophecy must always align with God's Word. Much of the prophecy today is speaking the prophetic message that Jesus proclaimed. Matthew 24 and Luke 21, contains Jesus prophetic messages concerning the end time.

Teaching is a talent given to some members of the church. It is one thing to learn a subject well; it is another to learn it well enough to teach it to others. A good teacher of God's Word is indispensable to explain its meaning and truth.

We encourage people to read their Bibles, but yet for so many it is hard to understand what the message is. It is good to have a teacher who can explain the message of the Bible.

Serving is what Christians do. They follow the example of Jesus, who even washed people's feet. This action was significant in his cultural context, as it was always the servant of the house who washed the feet of the guests. Jesus' ultimate act of serving was dying on a cross for humanity. Christ doesn't want his Church to be an entertaining Church, a consumer Church, a business Church, or a club; but rather, the Church that serves. Everyone in the church is a participant. It is not like a ball game where you have a few people on the court while everyone else sits back and watches critically. In the Church, everyone is on the court doing the work. The more servants, the stronger the mission and the ministry of that Church will be. We may go into a Church as a consumer expecting to be entertained, but if that Church is preaching the gospel, our hearts will be changed and we will come out carrying our cross and ready to serve. The purpose of a Church is to worship the risen Jesus Christ, receive His salvation, and be empowered to go out into the world as humble servants. Jesus' Church is a servant Church, and is always sacrificing for His causes. Just as Simon of Cyrene started out as a spectator as Jesus was carrying his cross to Mt. Golgotha, he soon found himself carrying the cross of Jesus part of the way there. Jesus expects us to join in the procession home to eternal life, and we are carrying the cross on the journey.

The Church both represents Jesus in the world and serves Jesus, whose image is reflected by those in need. It is Jesus serving Jesus. Jesus identifies with the poor, the sick, and the oppressed in society. Jesus said, "For I was hungry and you gave me something to eat. I was thirsty and you gave me something to drink. I was a stranger and you invited me in. I needed clothes and you clothed me. I was sick and you looked after me. I was in prison and you came to visit me...whatever you did for one of the least of these brothers of mine, you did for me." (Matthew 25:35-40) It is the Church of Jesus who serves the Jesus in our midst.

Encouragement is something that we all need. The world can say, "You are not good enough, you are not attractive enough, you are not strong enough, and you are not intelligent enough." As a result people suffer from low self-esteem. We all need encouragement, just as God encouraged Joshua before he led God's people into the Promised Land, "Be strong and courageous, because you will lead these people to inherit the land I swore to their forefathers to give them." (Joshua 1:6)

Encouragement will bring out the best in people. Words of encouragement will make a person confident to try. When a person tries, he will often succeed at what he is doing. He will begin somewhere, and learn as he goes. It is important to pray for people, praise them, and do what we can to equip the Christian workers with all they need to do the ministry assignment.

Contributing our financial means to the Church will help our mission and ministry thrive. There are always so many ministry needs of the Church, and our offerings go to support them. I have heard people mistakenly say, "All the Church wants is my money!" But really, what our Lord wants is you! We can give of our entire selves: our time, our talents, and our possessions for the work of the Church. We will always find a way to contribute to the things we believe in and have passion for.

Leadership is essential in the Church. A leader has the vision of what God wants the Church to be doing. A big part of this is spending time with God in prayer, and also listening to the needs and concerns of the people. A leader conducts the affairs of the church in an orderly manner. This person is able to work through conflict issues, but also be a motivator for the people. A good leader will work to draw in and include as many people into the ministry as he can.

Mercy is the value of the Christian Church. The simple prayer, "Lord, have mercy on me" is considered to be the oldest Christian prayer. It is the simple prayer that we pray daily. "Lord, have mercy on me to forgive me!" "Lord, have mercy on me to save me." "Lord, have mercy to direct me." God showed His incredible mercy by sending His son, Jesus, to die for us. As God is merciful to us, we are to be merciful to one another. When the immense weight of sin has been lifted from us, we have the Holy Spirit come and fill our hearts and minds with Christ Jesus. When we see a brother or sister whose back is against the wall, we do not pummel the person, but show mercy on them. It is out of deep hurt that we find compassion, and it is out of this compassion that we show mercy to others.

The Church is the product of the Holy Spirit, and continues the stewardship of proclaiming the Word of God, and administering the sacraments. The Holy Spirit inspires the Church to do the work of Jesus in the world.

Just as in the familiar story of the Good Samaritan, Jesus is the one who finds us on the side of the road, half dead and beaten down by the Devil. He restores our strength through His selfless act of mercy, and now calls us to do likewise. He calls us to be people who show love, mercy, and compassion for others in need.

Prayer is communicating to God who is our loving Heavenly Father. As we pray to the Heavenly Father for the Holy Spirit, God promises to send the Holy Spirit to us. "If you then, though you are evil, know how to give good gifts to your children, how much more will your Father in heaven give the Holy Spirit to those who ask him!" (Luke 11:13)

As we pray, and are filled with the Holy Spirit, God awakens and enlightens us to His presence, His purposes for our lives, and He puts us to work, working for the causes of Jesus in this world. God calls us to stay awake and watch. We do this through prayer and studying God's Word. What is it that we are to be seeing? It is more like going to the movie theater to watch a movie. As we watch, we see the story unfold before our eyes. When we pray, we will see God's purposes and plans unfold before our very eyes. "For I know the plans I have for you. Plans to prosper you and not to harm you, plans to give you hope and a future." (Jeremiah 29:11)

Questions
1. What is the impetus of the Christian life?
2. Where is Heaven?
3. How do we receive the Holy Spirit?
4. What is the work of the Holy Spirit?
5. What is the difference between the work of the Holy Spirit and behavioral psychology?
6. How are we bonded as Christians?
7. What role did you have in your nuclear family as a child? Do you find yourself in those same roles today?
8. How does Apostle Paul illustrate the church?
9. What gifts do you have to serve God and the Church with?
10. How are you an active participant in the Church?

GENEROSITY

Greed and Generosity always begin with a capital "G". They both are gigantic. Greed is a great pouring into one's self; while generosity is a great outpouring from one's self. It is always good to have generous people around, while it is destructive to have greedy people around us.

As a child in the late 1960's and early 1970's, I loved to play ball games with my friends at a local schoolyard. Across from the field where we played was a full-service gas station. They had a mechanic working in the shop, a little store with auto supplies, and most interestingly to us, some candy and soda pop machines. One day I took a break from our game and went across the street to purchase a candy bar, which cost only 10 cents at the time. As I put my dime into the machine, I pulled the lever to receive my "$100,000" candy bar. To my delight, the machine not only dispensed one candy bar, but three came out! I pulled the lever again, and it gifted me a few more. I did this a number of times. In my young mind, I'd hit the ultimate jackpot. I returned across the street and was about to share the bounty with my friends, when my brother asked, "Where did you get those?" I explained what happened. He admonished, "Bring those back to the gas station, that is stealing!" The store owner smirked as my brother made me hand the candy bars back to him. I'd been so sure it was my lucky day.

Another day, I took a break from playing and went across the street to the filling station, this time in search of soda pop. Back then one can cost 25 cents. I put my quarter into the machine, and got nothing in return. I told the owner of the gas station what happened, and he returned my quarter.

Gambling is much like this. Either the machines are taking our money, or they are dispensing money that really doesn't belong to us. We give a minimum input, somehow expecting a maximum output. The scales of gambling are tilted in such a way, making it an unfair contest. So it is with society, when the scales of justice are unbalanced, this causes discord and hardship. So much division in communities, and wars amongst nations are brought on because of injustice. A greedy spirit does this. This is why I don't gamble; it will develop a character of greed within me.

My second year of seminary, there was a very rich and benevolent man who supported me financially. One day as we had lunch together in a café, I noticed three waitresses jostling in position to wait on our table. Their excitement was obvious. We ordered our hamburger basket meals, which in the 1980's cost a total of ten dollars. As we were leaving, I noticed this generous man leave a $100 tip for the waitress. Now I understood why all the waitresses were wanting to serve us.

As a young boy, popsicles cost 10 cents. I asked my dad if I could have two dimes, so that my friend and I could purchase popsicles at the store. My father gave me one dime. I looked at him and said, "Aren't you also going to give a dime to my friend?" My dad said, "Split it." I responded, "Split it! How can I split a dime?" My father said, "Buy a popsicle with the dime, and then split it." Popsicles had two haves. That day, my father taught me how to split a dime, and the value of sharing.

Naboth's Vineyard

1 Kings 21, tells the story of two ruthless people. They were King Ahab and Queen Jezebel, king and queen of Israel. What made them so ruthless was their greed-centered characters. They had so much land in the kingdom, yet that wasn't enough for them. Their neighbor, Naboth, had a little vineyard adjacent to King Ahab's land. Ahab wanted to have this little vineyard for himself. He offered to pay Naboth or even give him a better parcel of land, but for Naboth the land was not for sale, because it was priceless to him. The land had been in Naboth's family for many generations, and family roots for Naboth ran very deep, so he didn't want to take up Ahab's offer. Ahab sulked around until Queen Jezebel exclaimed, "You are the king, man up!" Jezebel plotted against Naboth, and had him put to death. Because of her greedy action, God's judgment came to King Ahab's family.

The nature of greed is much like playing a game of Monopoly. There are properties on the board that go from lesser to greater value. This creates a class system of lower, middle, and high social classes. As players progress in the game, everyone seems to be doing fine until one player is able to make some trades, purchase houses or hotels, and accumulates money on unfortunate people who cannot pay rent as they land on the player's property. In time, one person will own the whole board. We observe the same with economies throughout the world. If people have greed, and governments cannot regulate their economic system, soon the wealth of the people will be in the hands of a few. We are living in such a time in history. Jesus said, "What good is it for a man to gain the whole world, yet forfeit his soul?" (Mark 8:36) It is only God who can satisfy life. When we have Jesus as our savior, we are content and thankful. Otherwise, we hunger for the things of this world to satisfy us. The whole world cannot satisfy our soul, only God can. Jesus said, "I am the bread of life. He who comes to me will never go hungry and he who believes in me will never be thirsty." (John 6:35)

Rich Young Man

In Matthew 19:16-26, we hear the story of a rich young man who wonders what he must do to receive eternal life. This man is into doing, so Jesus asks him if he has been following the commandments of God, and the man indeed seems to be following them. Jesus responds, "Only God is good." With this reply, Jesus is teaching that only God can save. Religion can be so legalistic, and in our preoccupation with following rules, we mistakenly search for the minimum requirement for salvation. Jesus is trying to show a life without limits. He is concerned not with the minimum to fulfill a requirement, but with the maximum outpouring of God's spirit in life.

I remember as a student on the first day of school, my classmates would always be pressing our teachers to figure out the minimum requirement to get an A in the class. Our instructors always seemed disappointed by this. In one psychology class, there was a student who did all that the professor required, but would also read extra books and do her own research on the subject. She wasn't concerned with getting an A (although that was her grade), but with learning as much about the subject as she could.

That is what Jesus is emphasizing with this rich young man: maximize your life. Go beyond the legal minimums, and live a life filled with the Holy Spirit of God. Your life will be a generous outpouring of godliness.

Jesus encouraged the man to give up all of his worldly wealth, and be filled with the riches of God's grace. Jesus offered this man life, and he turned it down. Everyone thought of him as being so exemplary in life. If he can't be saved, then who can? With God all things are possible. It is in Jesus Christ that we have salvation.

Zacchaeus

As we read in Luke 19:1-9, we hear the story of Zacchaeus. Zacchaeus was a very wealthy man, a chief tax collector in fact. Tax collectors during this time were notorious for cheating people by charging more taxes than what they owed and pocketing the difference.

As Jesus went into Jericho, he visited Zacchaeus's house. I don't know what he said to Zacchaeus, but it brought spiritual transformation to his life. Zacchaeus repented of his sins and turned to a life of freedom and generous giving. He gave half of his wealth to the poor, and even repaid back four times those whom he defrauded. Zacchaeus received the salvation of God, and was able to experience a fulfillment that riches could not provide. This is the transforming power of the Holy Spirit working from the inside out.

First Fruits and Tithes

Christian giving is without limits, yet it's always a good idea to have disciplines and goals to work toward. In the books of Leviticus and Deuteronomy, the Israelites are instructed to give their "first fruits." In other words, give to God first. They would give their first harvest to God, trusting that more harvests would follow. This shows God that we trust Him as a provider. In 1 Corinthians 15, otherwise known as the "resurrection chapter," Paul refers to Jesus as the first fruits of the resurrection. (1 Corinthians 15:20) Jesus is the first fruits, but there will be a great harvest of souls to follow, as people receive Jesus as savior.

As previously discussed, there is also the discipline of tithing, or giving 10% of our income to the work of the Lord. We must always remember that God has given us 100%. As God works in our lives, His generosity knows no limit.

Wrong Motivations

If every member of the Church gave 10% of their income to the Lord's work, Christ's Kingdom would provide for all the needs of the world. Even if they all gave 5%, that would make a huge impact on their community and world.

When people do not want to give, they resort to gimmicks like raffles and other fundraisers asking the community to support their church. This is backwards. The church supports the community, and not the other way around. People are greedy. They are expecting a lot for nothing, and think they are doing a generous work for the church. An offering is a sacrifice cheerfully given. We give our offerings to God with no strings attached.

I remember being at a Bible camp that was having a huge quilt auction. People made beautiful quilts and donated them to the Bible camp. One lady bid $500 and won a quilt. She took the quilt and hugged it. She was the person who sewed the quilt. The quilt was worth $1500. She wasn't going to allow all of her hard work to be sold for a fraction of what it was worth. That was the shame of the day; people were buying quilts for a fraction of what they were worth, and then thinking they were doing a good thing by supporting the Bible camp. This was an exercise of greed. People were getting a lot for a little of nothing. Be generous and give your tithes!

Some people have the attitude of what I call, "boomerang giving." As they give, they have a string attached to their giving. They do not see their offering as something sacrificed to the Lord, but rather something that will benefit them in return. They will designate their offering to support a project that will benefit them personally, rather than looking outside of themselves and supporting the causes of Christ in the world. This motivation stems from seeing the Church as an exclusive club that supports the internal causes concerning its members exclusively.

Another example of a selfish motivation for giving would be for tax breaks. If the government is requiring me to give a percentage of my income to charitable organizations as a tax break, then I will only give according to what the government sets as the amount.

A Christian always wants to be motivated by the Holy Spirit to give generously for the purposes God has called us to serve. It is an exciting adventure. The more we grow in our faith, the more generous we become. We find that our life is bound in God. God becomes greater in our lives, and self becomes lesser. This is the full life that is abundant in God's love and grace.

God has blessed us to be a blessing. Maximize your living by being that generous blessing to the church. There is great joy in giving. The "JOY" principle is putting Jesus first, Others second, and Yourself third.

Questions
1. What is the tension between generosity and greed?
2. What is the tragedy of Naboth's story?
3. What is the tragedy of the rich man?
4. How much worldly wealth do we need to be content?
5. What is the legal limit of generosity?
6. What was the good news of Zacchaeus' story?
7. What does it mean to give our "first fruits"?
8. What are wrong motivations for giving?
9. Does the community support the Church or does the Church support the community?
10. How are you challenged in your giving?

TIME

TIME IS OUR GREATEST commodity because we all have a limited amount of it. We cannot put a price tag on its value. Some people earn millions of dollars every year and have enough money to last many lifetimes. The problem is they only have one lifetime to spend it. As such a precious resource, time is even more valuable than money, so much so that people will often give money to causes in lieu of giving their time. Since we only have a limited amount of time, we will use it for our greatest value.

The Light of Life

Jesus said, "You are going to have the light just a little while longer. Walk while you have the light, before darkness overtakes you. The man who walks in the dark does not know where he is going. Put your trust in the light while you have it, so that you may become sons of light." (John 12:35-36)

Light represents life, and Jesus is the light of the world. A day is like a life in itself. The sun rises in the morning, it reaches its pinnacle height during midday, and then it sets. As a pastor, I have officiated a few funerals for babies who only lived one precious day. As I reflect on this, if I were granted only one day as an adult, how would I live it? Would I spend the day complaining, "This isn't fair, I only get one day to live!" Would I say, "I only have one day, what's the use!?" and waste it? Or, I could start the day in prayer asking God to come into my life. I could live my one day for God's plans and purposes. In the morning, I would make a plan of what I wanted to accomplish in the day, and then spend most of it working on the plan. At a certain time of the day, I would take a break to do something I enjoy, such as going for a run. As the sun sets on my day, I would give God thanks for it. It is important to approach everyday with this attitude. This way, all of our days together become a life dedicated to God. We will be making the most of each day, not wasting even one. We will be wise stewards of the time God has given us.

Transforming Light

I once lived in a community that was hit by a tornado. Fortunately, no one was killed, but there was massive destruction of buildings and trees throughout our entire town. A few minutes of a tornado can make for a whole year's worth of work and recovery. To begin with, there was so much to clean up and the power in our community was out for a couple of days. While there was light outside, we could work like beavers clearing away fallen trees and debris, but the setting sun and complete darkness to follow would put an abrupt stop to our efforts. At home, I would habitually flip the light switches whenever I entered a room, only to be greeted by more gloom and shadows. As soon as the first rays of dawn would pierce the dark sky, work could resume. During this experience I realized just how valuable light is.

Life has its daybreak. As we grow older we have our time to blossom and bloom under the sun, and eventually the time comes when the sun will set on our days. We want to make the most of our days. We do not want to live in the darkness, but rather we want the light of Jesus to drive out all the evil. It is important that we repent of evil, and be transformed by the Holy Spirit.

Apostle Paul writes, "For you were once darkness, but now you are light in the Lord. Live as children of light (for the fruit of light consists in all goodness, righteousness and truth) and find out what pleases the Lord. Have nothing to do with the fruitless deeds of darkness, but rather expose them. For it is shameful even to mention what the disobedient do in secret. But everything exposed by the light becomes visible, for it is light that makes everything visible. This is why it is said: 'Wake up, O sleeper, rise from the dead, and Christ will shine on you.' Be very careful, then, how you live- not as unwise, but as wise, making the most of every opportunity, because the days are evil. Therefore do not be foolish, but understand what the Lord's will is. Do not get drunk on wine, which leads to debauchery. Instead, be filled with the Spirit. Speak to one another with psalms, hymns, and spiritual songs. Sing and make music in your heart to the Lord, always giving thanks to God the Father for everything, in the name of our Lord Jesus Christ." (Ephesians 5:8-10) God has given us an allotted amount of days to live in relationship with Him. We want to do our best to please and glorify His name. We do not want to be foolish with the precious time that God has given. We are to be filled with the Holy Spirit every day, so we may be filled with the joy of His presence. When someone is singing or whistling a song, this is always a good sign of God's presence in a person's life. We can waste our time being slothful, drunk, or sexually immoral; or we can be productive in our lives worshipping, serving, and having fellowship in Jesus' name.

Boundaries

I hear people say, "I don't have time for God and the Church." They don't have anything against God, but have gotten so involved in the world's demands that they no longer have time for

God. We have all the time, but we need to prioritize it for the things that we most value. Once we have figured out what we truly value, then we will use our time optimizing that value.

As we set our value priorities we also need to set boundaries. The boundary will help us say "no" to the things we don't value, so we will have the time and resources left to say "yes" to the things that we do value. God is always our highest value, so we will take the time to align ourselves with Him. We find our joy in the Holy Spirit, so we do not have to resort to alcohol. We desire to work on God's kingdom, so we are productive. We are seeking the highest godly value in our relationships, so we do not resort to sexual immorality.

A Healthy Balance

Jesus said, "'Love the Lord your God with all your heart and with all your soul and with all of your mind.' This is the first and greatest commandment. And the second is like it: 'love your neighbor as yourself.' All the Law and the Prophets hang on these two commandment." (Matthew 22:37-40) God has created us with three parts to our person: A body, a mind, and a spirit.

God has given us a **body.** The body is our earthly tent. When we exercise, eat right, and get an adequate amount of sleep, we feel so much better. It is important to take at least 30 minutes a day to exercise our bodies, and to have a balanced diet of meats, fruits, breads, and vegetables. It is also important to get close to eight hours of sleep a night. When we fail to get exercise, eat too much junk food, and lack sleep, we get depressed. Remember our bodies are the temples of the Holy Spirit. This does not mean that the Holy Spirit will only dwell in physically fit people, but a physically fit body will make us feel good, and keep us strong to do God's work.

It is very important to exercise our **minds**. We are what we think. Wherever our mind is, then that is where we will be. It is important to educate our minds, and to stretch our minds to grow. The more we know, the better off we will be. Our minds help us to put reason to our faith. As we take steps in faith, we grow in our knowledge of God. As we grow in our knowledge of God, we develop a deeper relationship with God, with Creation, and with others.

It is important that we take the time to exercise and stimulate our minds everyday, and learn about the things that we are interested in. Some people enjoy learning about nature, others love history, and others like literature. Some enjoy analytical things such as mathematics, mechanics, and physics. Taking courses and having a good teacher can help expand our minds in ways we wouldn't have otherwise imagined. For example, a college student may reluctantly take an elective on a subject that she would never have thought about studying, only to find that the professor made the subject so interesting that she decides to change her major.

God has given to us a **spirit, or soul**. This is the part of our person that hungers and thirsts for God. We connect with God by receiving His Holy Spirit, hearing His Word, and receiving the Holy Sacraments. We are overflowing with the grace-filled life of the resurrection of Jesus. We experience pardon and peace, receive inspiration and motivation, and have an outpouring of fruitful living.

We are living in a world that is becoming more and more robotic. Even I converse with a couple of robots each day such as Alexa and Siri. I can ask them almost any question and they are able to tell me answers and give me very good information. However, when I ask them spiritual questions such as, "Do you believe in God?" They responded by saying, "I don't have an opinion about that." Most robots have a body and they also have a mind that can think on a very high level, but they do not have a soul that can interact with God. As I think about life without God, we have a body and we have a mind, but we are living like robots. Yet God has created us with a soul, and if our soul is not interacting with God, then it will interact with other things. This is not God's design for life.

When we rebel against God, we try to fill the spiritual void with things like alcohol, sexual immorality, and worldly goods. We are not optimizing the spiritual potential that God wants us to have. It is in spiritual discipline that we devote our lives to God as we worship, pray, and serve Him with all of our hearts. It is important that we take the time each day to pray and spend time in God's Word.

There is one other part to a healthy balance, and that is the second part of Jesus' command. We are to love our neighbor as ourselves. If we only focus on ourselves as individuals, this can lead to selfish, inward thinking. Jesus teaches that as we grow in our relationship with God in body, mind, and spirit, we are to live out our faith in fellowship with the Christian Church and our service to others. This will give us the fulfillment and sense of purpose in life.

If you take a healthy person and isolate him, it won't take long before that person becomes maladjusted. It is very healthy that a person is connected and interacting with other people, as God wants us to share our lives with others. As we develop a healthy balance for life, we also have a healthy balance with our fellowship with other Christian believers.

As we interact with other believers, we have our uncompromising core values of love, forgiveness, compassion, kindness, and having a servant attitude. In the Church there are others who will share in your core values, pray for you, work with you, and keep you accountable. We are always the strongest and healthiest when we take time to be together.

TIME

Questions

1. Why is time our greatest commodity?
2. If you had one day to live, how would you live it?
3. How is life like a day?
4. Who gives us transforming light to drive out darkness?
5. How might we waste our days?
6. Why is it important to set good boundaries?
7. How do you take care of your body?
8. How are you exercising your mind?
9. What is our spirit/soul?
10. Why is being connected to the church part of a healthy life balance?

SOCIETY

PSYCHOLOGY IS THE STUDY of the mind or of the individual person, while sociology is the study of groups of people. Whenever there are two or more people, we are focusing on society and how people interact with each other.

We all belong to the human race. It is God's intention that we all have loving fellowship with Him, that is why He has created us, and we all are to be in loving fellowship with each other. We all have things in common. We all breathe the air. We all need to eat and drink. We all have to sleep. All of humanity has a commonality. Humanity also has its differences, and too often we find the difference to be a threat. Instead of appreciating our diversity, we develop prejudices toward those who are different than us.

Why is there still evil?

As I preach, "Christ is arisen from the dead!" There are those who say, "That is good news, but if this is the case, then why are there still so many problems? Why is there so much evil in the world? The Devil seems to be prowling around like a lion devouring everything in his path!" These are valid questions. God did not intend for our world to be filled with evil. It is out of love that God sent Jesus into the world to suffer the pain on the cross for our sins. God created us in love, and it is His intention that we have a relationship with Him based on love. God gave Adam and Eve, humanity's first parents, the choice to live in a loving relationship with Him or apart from Him. God placed the Tree of Knowledge of Good and Evil in the paradise Garden of Eden. We may ask, "Isn't this reckless of God? What if they choose to rebel?" It is not reckless, but rather a loving gesture. God doesn't want a relationship based on force, coercion, or manipulation, not any more than we would want relationships based on anything other than love. We wouldn't want a relationship with someone who threatens, "You better be my friend or I'll punch you in the face" or even, "I will give you a dollar a day if you'll be my friend." We also do not want to be in a controlling relationship where we are puppets on a string.

Humanity has chosen to live apart from God. The original temptation is to try to be God, and that is our original sin. We all want to be God. We want to have autonomy of self. We don't want anyone, including God, to tell us how to live our lives. This has placed humanity on a track whose train is heading for a ravine. Worse than that, the ravine is Hell. The nature of sin is that it does itself in. The good news is, God has sent Jesus who suffered and died on the cross, and on the third day was raised from the dead. God now offers to us life in Jesus Christ, but humanity's train continues to roar down the tracks, picking up more and more momentum. This course will continue until either sin self-destructs or more mercifully, when Christ comes again. Jesus said, "Therefore keep watch, because you do not know on what day your Lord will come." (Matthew 24:41) In these times, God wants us to be patient in our waiting and watching. God wants us as his Church to watch as we pray, as we worship, and as we serve the Lord in our lives.

Sin's Destructive Nature

Today, humanity's existence is threatened in various ways. The first is war. Is humanity anymore sinful today then it was at the beginning? No, but our weapons have progressed to where we are now capable of destroying the world in minutes. This is why it is important for the world leaders to turn to Jesus, the Prince of Peace, who commands us to love each other.

A second way that humanity's existence is being threatened is through climate change or global warming. All scientists around the world are in agreement that there is global warming as a result of humanity emitting carbon dioxide into the atmosphere. Humanity is called to be the stewards of the Earth, but instead we are destroying it. This is why it is imperative that humanity works on developing renewable energies, and work to conserve the soil, water, air, and other natural resources.

A third way is the lack of human value. God has placed humanity to be stewards of the Earth. God has given humanity a role to play in Creation and life. We all have a working purpose in Creation. God has given all the materials and resources, but has left a part for humanity to play. God has given us healing, but has given the physician a part to play. God has given us knowledge, but has given the teacher a role in education. God has given materials for building, but has given the builder a role to play. God has given life, yet has given us the important role of parenting. God has given us seeds, rain, sunshine, and soil, but has given the farmer a role in sowing and harvesting.

With the continued development of robotics, humanity's sense of worth is being taken away. A robot now is taking over the human element. The robot works hard all day, and it doesn't get sick, take breaks, or slow down. This is going to affect humanity in an adverse way.

Humanity has developed theories to eliminate God from their lives. By doing this we have lost our soul. We no longer draw life from the giver of life. God gives us the eternal love, joy, and hope that only He can provide. He is the difference between us being living beings or robots. Robots can think at a high level, and can be built with amazing strength, but they have no soul. As people develop an atheistic perspective of Creation and life, the spiritual aspect has been diminished, and people become like robots with a body and mind, but no soul. As humanity develops its relationship to modern technology, such as computers and smartphones, we lose our relational value with each other. We no longer have the spiritual connectedness to God and to one another, which poses a huge threat to human existence. People no longer desire the fellowship and concern for each other, but now are in communion only with their electronics that now bring a depersonalization of humanity.

Adam and Eve had two sons named Cain and Abel. Cain killed Abel. When God confronted Cain about this, Cain's defensive argument was, "Am I my brother's keeper?" That is just it, Cain. You *are* your brother's keeper! Just as we rebelled against God and don't want God as part of humanity, we also do not see ourselves in a loving and caring relationship to one another. As we live our lives, there is a ripple effect that goes out into the world. Our ripple can have a loving effect or a destructive effect on the rest of humanity.

God Brings Order

When God created the universe he brought order out of chaos by applying physical laws to Creation. Just as God has created order to the physical universe, so God brings order to society. God has instilled the Ten Commandments to bring order for society. Humanity needs a common value system that we all can adhere to. God gives humanity a template to base truth, right from wrong. How do we know right from wrong? Who sets the standard? If one person has a moral standard, and another one has a different standard, whose opinion matters? If one person thinks that murder is right, while another person thinks that murder is wrong, who is the judge? This is why we need a focal point that is higher than humanity, and that is God. He sets the standard. I have known judges and law enforcement officers who have said, "So much of the grounds of our work are based on the commandments of God."

Government

Apostle Paul writes, "Everyone must submit himself to the governing authorities, for there is no authority except that which God has established. The authorities that exist have been established by God. Consequently, he who rebels against the authority is rebelling against what God has instituted, and those who do so will bring judgment on themselves. For rulers hold no terror for those who do right, but for those who do wrong. Do you want to be free from fear of the one in authority? Then do what is right and he will commend you. For he is God's servant to do you good. But if you do wrong, be afraid, for he does not bear the sword for nothing. He is God's servant, an agent of wrath to bring punishment on the wrongdoer. Therefore, it is necessary to submit to the authorities, not only because of possible punishment but also because of conscience. This is also why you pay taxes, for the authorities are God's servants, who give their full time to governing. Give everyone what you owe him: If you owe taxes, pay taxes; if revenue then revenue; if respect, then respect; if honor, then honor." (Romans 13:1-7)

God has instituted government. God has given to people the stewardship of the Church, but also the government. Government has been instilled by God to legislate just laws, protect the people, and provide infrastructure: roads, education, water works, and other important amenities. The English Philosopher, John Locke said, "All people have the right to life, liberty, and the pursuit of happiness." Good government will allow this to happen. Just as God has called pastors and leaders in the Church, so God has called government leaders. They are all to be above reproach and set a good moral example to the people.

There is separation between church and state, but yet they are to work hand in hand. The Church proclaims the gospel that brings forgiveness and eternal life, and instills the hope and promise of the resurrection. We live in the victory of our Lord Jesus Christ. The Church proclaims the risen Jesus until he comes again.

Just as we give our offerings to support the Church, it is very important to pay our taxes to support the good work of the government. Jesus said, "Give to Caesar what is Caesar's and to God what is God's." (Mark 12:17)

Justice and Peace

"Love and faithfulness meet together; righteousness and peace kiss each other." (Psalm 85:10) God is the one who has established just scales. Jesus' cross stands for reconciliation, justice, and peace. As we bring our injustice and guilt before the cross, He brings pardon and peace.

Justice means being fair. Things are made of an equal exchange. One person pays another a monetary sum for quality of work or the value of an item. When both people feel as though they got a fair exchange in life, then there is peace. When the scales of justice are imbalanced, then that creates an escalating discord that leads to division and war.

When a society is at peace, then it can prosper. People can go to work and support their families, children are able to go to school and become educated, and people can pursue their dreams. For example, Europe has had seventy years of prosperity because its many nations have remained at peace. Some countries remain underdeveloped because they cannot maintain peace long enough to build infrastructure.

Injustice angers God. It brings division among nations, races, and social classes. God wants us to strive for justice and peace in

SOCIETY

the world. You cannot have one without the other; they need to be in a harmonious kiss. God spoke through the prophet Amos, "But let justice roll on like a river, righteousness like a never-failing stream!" (Amos 5:24)

Questions

1. What is a society?
2. Why did God create humanity?
3. Why is there still evil?
4. How is humanity's existence restored?
5. What role does humanity play in Creation and life? What is your role?
6. How does God bring order to Creation and society?
7. What is the role of government?
8. What did John Locke feel are humanity's God given rights?
9. Why must justice and peace "kiss"?
10. How does God restore justice?

WORK

IT IS OUT OF pain that we produce the output of our work, and it is out of pain that we have life. As we read in Genesis 3:16-17, following the fall of humanity, God placed a curse on Adam (men), and Eve (women). The curse for women will be that they will have to suffer much pain in childbirth, and for men, they will have to suffer hard labor as they provide for their families. As we suffer the pains of these curses, we must remember that God has also brought us blessings. Although a mother endures excruciating labor, she experiences a greater joy in holding her baby. As a man suffers the strain of his work, he reaps the blessing of a successful harvest.

It is out of the cross that Jesus brings life. Jesus will come again. As it is written in Matthew 24, there will be much suffering and pain before Jesus comes, but Jesus said, "They are the birth pangs of a new life." (verse 8) We will suffer much in this world and life, but joy will come in the resurrection. We will experience the heavenly bliss of God's eternal kingdom, the release of all evil, and the joy of God's presence.

Jesus taught us to pray the Lord's Prayer. In this prayer there is a petition, "Give us this day our daily bread." Martin Luther's explanation of this petition, "God gives daily bread, even without our prayer, to all people, though sinful, but we ask in this prayer that he will help us to realize this and to receive our daily bread with thanks."

Breaking Bread

I had a great-aunt named Connie. She was the daughter of Norwegian immigrants and the oldest of their 13 children. Her parents passed away within a few years of each other, leaving behind 13 orphans, a few of them still in diapers. Normally, these children would have been placed in orphanages, but my then teenage Aunt Connie was determined to keep the family together and raise the younger children herself. She worked terribly hard to accomplish this, sacrificing time she should have spent studying and socializing just to keep everyone fed. My grandmother recalled watching her wake up early to knead the bread dough before rushing off to high school, and then stealing home from class during her lunch hour to quickly bake it.

As I was a young boy visiting her, we would sit down at the dinner table for the meal that she prepared. We would give thanks for the food, and as I was ready to take a bite of the bread, she would stop me saying, "Jesus broke the bread, so we must do the same." Her breaking the bread always reminded her of the pain and sacrifice that it took to have our daily bread, but yet how we celebrate with thanksgiving that we have the bread as a gift from God.

Jesus said, "I am the bread of life, he who comes to me will not hunger and he who believes in me will never be thirsty." (John 6:35) Jesus spoke these words after famously feeding 5,000 people by multiplying five loaves of bread and two fish. The original fish and loaves were gifts that a young boy offered Jesus. Jesus then took them and multiplied them to feed so many. Jesus can do the same with our humble offerings; He consecrates them and uses them to bless a multitude of people.

Apostle Paul writes, "The Lord Jesus, on the night he was betrayed, took bread, and when he had given thanks, he broke it and said, 'This is my body, which is for you, do this in remembrance of me.' In the same way, after supper he took the cup, saying, 'This cup is the new covenant in my blood; do this, whenever you drink it, in remembrance of me.'" (1 Corinthians 23-25) We offer our bread to God who consecrates it for sacramental purposes.

I once took a trip to Norway and visited an open-air museum. They had a house that dated back a couple of centuries. In the house, the main piece of furniture was a long table. My first question was, "How did they ever get the table into the house?" The museum guide explained that people would first build the table, and then build the house around it. The second question I had was, "They must have had large families, judging by the size of the table?" They did have large families, but the table was large enough to seat all of their friends and neighbors.

Our Lord sets His table, and the Church is built around it. It is at the Lord's table that we are all invited; there is room for all. It is there we receive our Lord's salvation and have fellowship as brothers and sisters in Christ.

Full Day's Pay

When my father would tell stories about what it was like growing up during the Great Depression in North Dakota, he would describe the scenes of hopelessness that became the new norm. He said, "Men would be sitting on benches on Main Street, hoping farmers would hire them as they were coming into town." People who are in such a desperate financial situation feel so fortunate to be hired even for a day. This would guarantee them a full day's pay to provide for their families.

In Matthew 20:1-16, Jesus tells the parable of a man who owned a vineyard. The vineyard is ripe for harvest, so he goes to the marketplace where people were hoping to be hired for a day.

Those who were chosen early in the morning would have peace, knowing that they would receive their full-day's pay to provide for all of their needs. As the day progressed, the owner continued to hire more workers as needed. Some were hired toward the very end of the day. This shows their level of desperation for income, as they were willing to work for even part of the day. Even a little of a day's pay is worth something.

At the end of the day, the owner gave a full day's pay to everyone, even those who worked just a few hours. Was this fair? Shouldn't those hired at the end of the day have been paid less, or those who worked the full day have gotten more? The owner was very generous. The owner represents God, and we are all His people. Some of us have been Christians our whole lives, while others have come to faith at a later time, but we all need the full day's pay of salvation. The full day's pay is Jesus. We all need Jesus for salvation, whether we have been in the vineyard of God's Church our whole life, or received Jesus toward the end of life. We are all called to labor as workers in Jesus' church.

Producing a loaf of bread requires a community. It is the farmer who sows the seeds and harvests the grain. It's the mill worker who mills the grain into flour. The baker makes bread from the flour. The truck driver transports the bread to the grocer, and the grocer finally sells it to the consumer. The loaf of bread is a gift from God, and so many people have been a part of this gift. So many people have jobs because of the loaf of bread. A community is formed by the one loaf of bread God provides for our daily bread, our full day's pay. The community in turn offers the loaf of bread to God. As the community gathers around the Lord's table, the loaf of bread is broken and the community receives the salvation of Jesus Christ. The community of God is unified as one while celebrating the diversity of its members, being the Church in the world.

Talents

Jesus tells the story in Matthew 25:14-30, of a man who goes on a journey entrusting his property to stewards. He gives five talents to one steward, two talents to another steward, and one talent to a third steward. The stewards who received the five talents and the two talents, both went out and doubled the talents. Each talent was worth approximately $1,000. The master of the talents was very pleased with their work saying, "Well done good and faithful servants."

The steward, who received the one talent, was afraid of losing it so he decided to bury it. The master was not pleased with him. The master was upset, because the steward didn't try.

God has entrusted us with Creation and life. God encourages us to try, as so much of success comes out of failure. Two things that we always need to remember are that we should always try, and that we must not have fear of failure. Just as God brought resurrection out of death, He will bring success out of failure. We learn from our failures, and we must have the courage to try again. Most often when a person tries, they will show fruit from their efforts. We always have to start somewhere. As we start, God gives us wisdom, guidance, and encouragement to keep going in times of discouragement.

It's important that we encourage one another. Faithful ministry that bears fruit is a result of people encouraging one another. By working together we can accomplish much, that is the strength of uniting as a Church in God's love. There are many talented people who amaze me with their abilities, but I am even further amazed by what the Church can do when we combine our efforts. Our talents are compounded and our productivity is beyond measure.

Vocation

Our vocations are always holy callings when we use the skills that God has given us to His glory. Apostle Peter writes, "But you are a chosen people, a royal priesthood, a holy nation, a people belonging to God, that you may declare the praises of him who called you out of darkness into his wonderful light. Once you were not a people, but now you are the people of God; once you had not received mercy, but now you have received mercy." (1 Peter 2:9-10) Clergy obviously have a sacred calling, yet all people have a holy calling when they use their gifts for the service of God and serving God in society. We gather to worship God, but then we are sent into society to live out our Christian callings in serving people in our vocations. We are blessed to have teachers, doctors, plumbers, electricians, homemakers, mechanics, factory workers, farmers, carpenters, etc., who are called to serve humanity. Do you see how special you are, and how important your work is? How blessed we are by your service!

We pursue vocations based on our personality types. Some people are outgoing socially, while others are more reserved. Some people like low-stress jobs, while others are always looking for the greatest challenge in life. Some people like to work indoors, while others want to work outdoors. Some people are stronger with literary, artistic, and musical skills, while others have more analytical skills and thrive while doing mechanical work.

When considering a vocation, we need to ask these questions:

1. Does the vocation glorify God?
2. Do I like doing this work?
3. Do I have the skills for this work? If not, where can I develop them?
4. Can I make a living at this vocation?
5. Does the vocation serve humanity?

We hone our talents through education, practice, taking advice from senior advisors, and experience. We can't have fear of failure, and we pray that God will give us the courage to try. God will bless our labor.

As mentioned earlier, God has given us the stewardship of work in caring for creation and society. The ability to work and the calling of a vocation is a special gift of God. God provides work for us. God provides for all that we need for daily life. God also provides that we may give our tithes and offerings to support the church as mentioned earlier. God has also blessed and provided for us through the government. We benefit from protection, just laws, infrastructure, schools, streets, fire department, and medical care. We are thankful that God provides through taxes to provide for the government. As we read Matthew 17:24-27, we hear the account of God providing for Jesus and Peter the four coins for them to pay their Temple taxes. Peter found the coins in the mouth of a fish he caught. Was the miracle of the coins that happened to be in the fish, or was it in Peter's vocation as a fisherman to catch fish? Peter could go to the market place, sell the fish and have the coins to pay his taxes. With Peter's God given ability to catch fish, God provides for all of his needs. God performs His miracles in and through the vocations that we perform in His service.

Skill Set

Developing our skill sets will allow us to be productive in our respective vocations, and we can often use the same skill set to serve the Church. While living in northern Wisconsin, I knew a man who was a senior plumber and electrician. He was a very skilled man, having served the community with his business for decades. He frequently volunteered, giving of his time and talents to our Church. One bitterly cold winter night, a very poor couple for whom lived far out in the country had their furnace fail. It was 2:00 a.m. when I called this man and asked if he could help the couple. He went out with me in the middle of the night and repaired the furnace. This is an example of a man who had a holy calling as he served God, his church, and his community.

The Sabbath

God gives the commandment, "Remember the Sabbath day and keep it holy." As we work in our professions, it's important to take one day off a week as our Sabbath rest. Our body, mind, and spirit need to recharge. This comes from resting, but also it gives people the opportunity to come together to hear God's Word, and receive the spiritual renewal that we hunger and thirst for. Taking a Sabbath rest is very important for self-care.

It is important that we take the time each day to read God's Word, and enjoy a hobby or interest that fills our cup. Some people will even develop an avocation. Avocations develop from interests that we develop based on our personalities, our settings in life, skills that we have, and the causes that we feel passionate about. It is important to spend time doing the things that we love.

Questions
1. Blessings often come through pain. Can you give some examples of this?
2. What are the curses and blessings in Genesis 3:16-17?
3. What does Jesus refer to the tribulation as being like?
4. What is the pain and blessing of bread?
5. How does producing bread require a community?
6. The Lord builds his Church around what?
7. What does it mean for you to have a full day's pay?
8. Why was God upset with the person with one talent?
9. How do you have a holy calling through vocation?
10. Why is it important to have a Sabbath day?

INVESTMENTS

JESUS TELLS THE PARABLE, "A farmer went out to sow his seed. As he was scattering the seed, some fell along the path, and the birds came and ate it up. Some fell on rocky places, where it did not have much soil. It sprang up quickly, because the soil was shallow. But when the sun came up, the plants were scorched, and they withered because they had no root. Other seeds fell among thorns, which grew up and choked the plants. Still other seeds fell on good soil, where they produced a crop- a hundred, sixty, or thirty times what was sown." (Matthew 13:3-8)

Investing seeds in good soil will produce a tremendous yield. Each seed has the potential of producing one hundredfold of itself. As the Holy Spirit cultivates the soil of our hearts and the seed of God's Word is planted in it, it too will produce the fruit of salvation. God produces a great harvest in Jesus, billions fold. God will produce a harvest of spiritual fruit in your life.

God has given 100% of Himself in Creation, and also the gift of His Son, Jesus Christ. We have 100% of the just requirement for salvation. Jesus is our righteousness. God has left nothing on the table, but rather has given everything. We have a loving and gracious Heavenly Father who cares very much for us.

Investments

Jesus said, "Do not store up for yourselves treasures on earth, where moth and rust destroy, and where thieves break in and steal. But store up for yourselves treasures in Heaven, where moth and rust do not destroy, and where thieves do not break in and steal. For where your treasure is, there your heart will be also... but seek first his kingdom and his righteousness, and all these things will be given to you as well." (Matthew 6:19-21; 33-34)

What are good investments? It seems hard to invest in a world that is decaying. Everything in this world is temporary. We can buy a nice, brand new car assuming it's a good investment only to find it reduced to rust 20 years later. As good stewards, it is important to maintain our automobiles, as well as other possessions. By doing this, we will get longevity from them. We are to work to preserve things as long as we can.

It is important to not live in the moment and be an impulse buyer, because we will spend a lot of money on things that we do not need. Using credit cards is not a good investment, because we will pay high interest on our purchases. We can also be tempted into thinking that gambling is a good investment, but the odds are not in our favor. We think we'll receive a maximum payoff for a minimal investment, when really the casino wins 97% of the time.

Investing in land is always a good investment. Land, like time, is limited. There is only a certain amount of land in this world, and it will only increase in value. Investing in stock mutual funds is another example of a good investment. A diverse portfolio will produce growth with interest over time.

Establishing a trust fund will continue to produce financially, but we must be patient. Aesop wrote a fable about the

Golden Eggs. A man had a goose that laid a golden egg. Soon it laid more and more, but the man became greedy and impatient. He couldn't wait for the goose to lay more golden eggs, so he killed the goose and removed what eggs were within her. After that, there were no more golden eggs. Money spends once, but if it is put in a trust fund, it will produce interest. The trust fund becomes like the goose that is laying golden eggs. We have to be patient as our investment generates interest. The temptation is to spend the trust fund, thus killing the "goose."

When we remember the Church when planning our will, we can bequest money to be given to a trust fund. Our money will continue to support the mission of God's kingdom on earth, long after we have entered God's kingdom in Heaven.

Seek First the Kingdom of Heaven

Jesus gives us godly advice when He says to invest our lives in God, because His kingdom is eternal. It is not subject to moths and decay. We must always set our priorities of seeking the kingdom of God first, because Jesus is our priceless treasure. Setting priorities will help us have the proper perspective in life. We will be able to set boundaries as to what is important versus what is not important. We will be wise in our decisions concerning investments, especially what we invest our lives in.

We are not going to invest our lives in something that we do not believe in. In John 20, we hear the story of Thomas, one of Jesus' disciples. Thomas was not present when Jesus appeared to the rest of the disciples. When the other disciples shared the great news of Jesus' resurrection, Thomas refused to believe until he saw the scars from the wounds Jesus suffered on the cross. When Jesus showed Thomas the scars of His hands and side; that is when Thomas worshipped Jesus and confessed him Lord and God of his life. The Holy Spirit will bring us to that same conviction as we study the Word of God. It is our conviction of Jesus being the arisen Lord that brings us to the commitment of following Him above all other things. Commitment will never exceed our faith. God will bless us with various gifts and talents based on our demonstration of faith. As we can be trusted with little, then He will trust us with more.

Jesus is the center of our lives, and He is the center of all other priorities. With Christ at the center of our lives, our priorities will be different. We invest in the Church, the kingdom of Heaven on earth. We invest in people. We invest in our families, our neighbors, and those who are in need. We invest in our communities and workplaces. We give our time, talents, and possessions to the things and people that we have a passion for. We have a passion for Jesus who calls us into Christian work.

Jesus said, "The thief comes only to steal and kill and destroy. I have come that they may have life, and have it to the full." (John 10:10) The Christian life is not so much a life of wealth, power, and pleasure, but rather, it is a life full of God. In God our lives are made complete. The Christian life is one that is being poured out into the lives of others. Love is what frees, and love is always something that is given. We experience the richness of God's presence and love in the filling of the Holy Spirit. The Holy Spirit's filling is one that overflows. The overflowing love of God is what brings compassion and release to the oppressed, the hurting, the poor, and the sick.

Discipline

It is important not to be impulse buyers, but rather set priorities based on our spiritual goals, and setting good boundaries. When we do this it will be easy to say, "No", to the things that do not fit into God's plan, and say, "Yes to the things that do."

It is important to differentiate between what are needs vs. wants. I may want to purchase a new snowmobile, but what I need is food on my table. When we ascertain our needs, then we prioritize and budget accordingly. It is nice to have wants, but we need to know the difference between wants vs. needs. It

INVESTMENTS

is tempting to extend our financial ability by using credit cards and bank loans to purchase items that we may or may not need. It is always healthy to live within our financial means. This may be hard, especially if the "Jones's" continue to flaunt all their worldly toys. What is important is to have a strong relationship with God. God is our joy. With God we find the contentment to enjoy the simple things of life, things that don't cost any money. Going for a walk on a beautiful day, or spending time with a special friend are examples of contentment. It is always important to be thankful for what we do have. Rather than being envious of others or always wanting more, we need to be thankful. We need to enjoy what we already have. A thankful attitude is always the remedy for envy and greed. When Jesus said, "If anyone would come after me, he must deny himself and take up his cross and follow me. For whoever wants to save his life will lose it, but whoever loses his life for me and for the gospel will save it." (Mark 8:34-35) The whole world cannot satisfy the soul. Only God can do that. We do now have people who own the whole world and are empty spiritually. It is when we experience the joy of salvation in Jesus, we are truly satisfied. We have gained the glory of God in Christ Jesus.

A little boy stuck his hand into a jar. The hand was stuck, and his mother was trying to help him free his hand from the jar. She noticed the boy's hand was in the shape of a fist. She said, "Release the fist then your hand will be freed from the jar." The boy responded, "Mother, I can't! If I do that, then I will lose my quarter." It is hard to lose our grip of the world, but when we do, we find our lives in God. It is in giving that we find blessings, but when we hold onto our blessings we only experience a curse.

As we read about the calling of Abraham in Genesis 12:1-3, God will bless he and his descendant, and they will be a blessing to all the nations. God would funnel His blessings in and through the Hebrew people. The ultimate blessing was the gift of the savior, Jesus. We are all called to share the blessings of

God generously with others. When we do this, we live; when we fail to do this, we die.

In the Holy Land, there are two seas: The Sea of Galilee and the Dead Sea. Water that is moving is fresh and life giving. The Sea of Galilee is such a body of water. The Sea has aquatic life. The Dead Sea has no outlet, so the water becomes saline. No aquatic life is able to live in this body of water. These two seas illustrate a point for our lives. Like the Sea of Galilee, when we share our blessings, we experience godly life, but like the Dead Sea, when we hoard blessings, we experience death.

God will bless our giving, and He will increase it. In John chapter 6, we hear the story of Jesus feeding the multitude. He took what a boy had, two fish and five loaves of bread. What was that in relation to feeding 5,000 people? Jesus takes what little we have, and uses it far beyond what we can imagine. As I was serving in a Church, I put out a basket called the Loaves and Fishes Basket. People were encouraged to bring nonperishable food items. Every week it didn't seem like much, but yet as needful people came for food, there always was enough. God provides through His people.

I knew a pastor who gave every member in attendance a five dollar bill. He said to the people, "You can keep it and spend it as you will, or you can be creative and see how you can make more money for the mission of the Church with it." People were creative, and many increased the five dollars to be a larger sum for the mission of the Church. An example of this was one person took the five dollars and made brownies with it. She then sold the brownies, multiplying the five dollars to 20 dollars. When we give our lives to the Lord, He will bless us to overflow with His goodness. It is in losing our lives, that we find our lives in Him. This may seem illogical to the worldly mind, but for those who take this step of faith, experience the abundance of God's presence in their lives.

Spending Life

In Luke 12:13-21, Jesus tells a parable about a man who was very successful. He had fields that produced bounteous harvests. He had so much grain that he didn't know what to do with it, so he kept building more and bigger barns. He was trying to gain worldly security so he would have abundance for the rest of his life.

In some ways, we would give this man high marks. He worked hard to produce wealth with what he was given, and he planned for a great nest egg in retirement. He would make his financial advisor proud. There was one problem though, that night he would die. Death is the big negative in life's equation. Death is a rip-off. It is so unfair.

As I look at this man's life, would we say that wealth is what we accumulate over life, or is wealth what we have given in life? This man had the ways and means to make a difference with his life in the world, but he failed to do it. All of this man's money had no power to save him, and he could not take it with him.

If you were to live only one day, and were given five dollars; what would you do with it? Would you keep the five dollars all day, or would you spend it? If you were to spend it, what would you value as being worth spending it on? Maybe you would give a dollar to support the mission of the Church. Maybe you would spend two dollars on your family. Maybe you would spend a dollar on a person in need, and maybe you would spend your last dollar on a cause that you have a passion for.

It is important to have a good financial plan, budget our income based on our valued priorities, and save for a possible retirement; but God has also called us to carry the cross of Jesus in our lives. We are to be living sacrifices, giving to the valued causes of Jesus.

Apostle Paul writes, "Therefore, I urge you, brothers in view of God's mercy, to offer your bodies as living sacrifices, holy and pleasing to God-this is your spiritual act of worship." (Romans

12:1) Worship is going before God's altar and dedicating our lives to Him. As we do, we are filled with God's love and salvation as we receive Jesus through the hearing of God's preached Word, and receiving the Holy Sacraments of Baptism and Communion. God then calls us to sacrifice ourselves in the world, as we share the blessings of salvation. We do this as we serve in our homes, our vocations, and our communities. As we come to worship, God fills and forms us like a beautiful grape; but then sends us out in the world where He crushes the grape, sending the blessings into the world. This is what it means to carry the cross of Jesus in our lives. We are blessed to be a blessing. We are filled and crushed as living sacrifices in our world.

When humanity fell to sin, it was Jesus who paid the debt in full, but yet our debt is to love others. The world is left parched by sin and lacking in love. The world needs love, and that is the Christians aim to always be flooding the earth with God's love, bringing life to the parched humanity.

When we live in the freedom of God's love and grace, we see life without limits. We no longer are living the minimal standards that we set for God, or give out of obligation. Instead, we are always seeing how we can give and spend our lives. The greatest joy is in our giving, and our giving is based on our thankfulness toward God. A thankful heart is not looking for minimal requirements, but rather sees the sky as the limit. As we grow in our faith in relationship to the Holy Spirit, there becomes less of self, and more of God. We no longer seek the things of this world, but we seek the kingdom of God and His righteousness. Greed weighs us down, but spiritual generosity uplifts our soul.

<u>Investment Battles</u>

We are to pray for God to inspire us, and call us to ministry ventures. Some of these ventures can be challenging. It is during these times that we are tempted to bury our talent in fear of losing it.

INVESTMENTS

As a pastor, I have led Churches into doing a lot of fruitful ministry. It has been exciting to see how God works through our church. One day, I was praying, asking God to show me what mission work He wanted our Church to be doing. The answer that God spoke to me was, "South Sudan." God called our church to build a school. Little did I know at the time that South Sudan would be given its freedom. I thought, "Perfect timing!" We gave a lot of money for the building of a boarding school for girls. Only a month after it was built, civil war broke out and the school was destroyed. I was horrified. I prayed to God in dismay, "I don't understand!" In time what I learned was, our mission was the girls. The people working in this ministry didn't miss a beat. They were making sure that the girls were now being kept safe in Uganda, so we continued to support their education there. Our investment was not so much in buildings, but rather the girls. Another message that God shared with me in my prayer was, "I am the God of the resurrection. I will raise the school up again one day." After the temple in Jerusalem was destroyed, God gave the promise of one day rebuilding the temple. That did happen. God promises to raise us up from the dead. Whenever we invest in God, it is an eternal investment: rust, moths, and even civil war cannot take it away. God will always bless our giving and work; He will multiply the investment. We will always be rich in God's love and mercy. His joy will overflow in our lives.

We invest in the kingdom of Heaven, and the kingdom's work that He has given to us. We may not see in a day the fruit of our labor, but we trust that God is going to bring the growth and the harvest. Apostle Paul wrote, "For what is our hope, our joy, or the crown in which we will glory in the presence of our Lord Jesus when he comes? It is not you? Indeed, you are our glory and joy." (1 Thessalonians 2:19-20)

As we grow in God's love and grace, we too sow the seeds that will provide a bountiful harvest. Apostle Paul writes, "Do not be deceived: God cannot be mocked. A man reaps what he sows.

The one who sows to please his sinful nature, from that nature will reap destruction; the one who sows to please the Spirit, from the Spirit will reap eternal life." (Galatians 6:7-8) We invest our lives in God's kingdom. We sow the seeds of God's Word, trusting in the certain hope that we will reap the bounty of His spiritual harvest.

Europe has many majestic cathedrals some of them took two hundred years to build. Those who started working on the cathedral did not see its completion. Then there were those who lived and worked on the cathedral at mid-point. They didn't see the work begin, nor did they see it end, but in faith they worked on the structure, trusting that one day it would be finished. We are called to be faithful to what God calls us to in our day. We are building on the Church's one foundation, Jesus Christ. We are picking up where the last generation left off, and the day comes when we will pass the work for the next generations. We must remember always that it is God who is the Alpha and Omega, the beginning and the end. He is the one who sees the big picture and He calls us to work in our time. We trust that, "God who began this good work will bring it to a completion on the day of Jesus Christ." (Philippians 1:6) We are called to be faithful stewards.

INVESTMENTS

Questions

1. Why are seeds so amazing?
2. What has God invested in you?
3. What are bad investments?
4. What are good investments?
5. Why are trust funds beneficial?
6. What is special about heavenly investments?
7. What do you invest in?
8. What is the lesson of the successful farmer?
9. If you had only one day to live and were given five dollars, what would you spend it on?
10. How are we to be faithful stewards?

BIBLIOGRAPHY

Aesop. Aesop's Fables. (New York: Doubleday, Page & Co, 1912).

Evangelical Lutheran Worship. (Minneapolis, Minnesota: Augsburg Fortress, Publishers, 2006).

Ketcham, Hank. Dennis The Menace. (Los Angeles: Hank Ketcham Enterprises, CBS Television. 1959-1963).

Luther, Martin. The Small Catechism. (Augsburg Publishing House/ Minneapolis and Fortress Press/Philadelphia. 1979).

The New International Bible. (Colorado Springs, Colorado. 1978).

www.ingramcontent.com/pod-product-compliance
Lightning Source LLC
Chambersburg PA
CBHW020015050426
42450CB00005B/475